# Junkers
# 1895–1969

**KEY** Books

AVIATION INDUSTRY SERIES, VOLUME 7

This edition © 2023

Published by Key Books
An imprint of Key Publishing Ltd
PO Box 100
Stamford
Lincs PE9 1XQ

www.keypublishing.com

Original editions published as *Aeroplane's Junkers Aircraft Company Profile 1895-1969* © *2013*, edited by Martyn Chorlton

All images are from Martyn Chorlton's collection, unless otherwise stated.

ISBN 978 1 80282 368 4



Typeset by SJmagic DESIGN SERVICES, India.

# Contents

# Introduction

Aged 56 by the time his first aircraft had flown, Professor Hugo Junkers can be described as one of the greatest aviation pioneers and a maverick to boot. His approach to how an aircraft should be built was like no other and, rather than modifying, re-designing or copying ideas from other pioneers, Junkers took his own unique route and doggedly stuck to it for the two decades. Proceeding in the face of the theory that aircraft should be built from wood and fabric, all Junkers aircraft, from the 'Tin Donkey' of 1915 onwards, were made of metal, a material that was regarded, right up to the early 1930s by many other aircraft manufacturers as being too heavy. Wood and fabric were of course ideal from a performance and massed production point of view, but Junkers was a visionary who had no ambition to make money on the back of military aircraft. His goal was to

**Junkers Ju 52 3/mte D-AGAK *Ulrich Neckel* pictured during peaceful service with Lufthansa. The aircraft would come to a violent end when, in February 1942, the airliner was shot down by Japanese fighters.**

prove that metal would display a much greater durability from a long-term commercial service point of view and his unceasing efforts to prove this also made Junkers and his aircraft as pioneers of the airline industry.

The Junkers aircraft story can be told in three parts; the first was under the control of the Hugo Junkers, the second by the Nazis until the end of World War Two and the final post-war period which saw the company exist as a remnant of its former self as part of MBB and the development of the re-usable spacecraft. The first part of the story is clearly dominated by Junkers efforts in production of commercial aircraft while the Nazi period, is unsurprisingly about military machines which help to rapidly re-build a new Luftwaffe. Only the iconic Ju 52/3m and the Ju 90 straddle these two periods of the company's history which initially contributed to advancement of aviation and finished by contributing to war. The pacifist, Professor Hugo Junkers, who died at the 76 in 1935, must have been turning in his grave when the skies were filled with aircraft in his name, waging war a few years later across Europe.

# The Junkers Story

**B**orn on February 3, 1859, in Rheydt, south of Mönchengladbach, Hugo Junkers was an incredible aviation pioneer who was first and foremost an engineer, entrepreneur and scientist but crucially, as time would tell, was not a natural businessman.

Following his general education, Junkers displayed a flair for all things relating to engineering and from 1878 he studied mechanical engineering at the Berlin Technical High School. Further studies on all available technical subjects were continued at the Rheinisch-Westfallen High School in Aachen between 1881 and 1883. A brief break from his studies saw him enjoy some work experience as a technical manager within his own father's mill in Rheydt, before he returned to Aachen in January 1884 to specialise in electrical engineering and thermodynamics. Junkers continued to gain work experience with a variety of engineering companies, but in June 1887 he returned to Berlin to expand his studies in electrical and mechanical engineering. At the tender age of 28, Junkers had already become a professor.

In 1888 his formal education now over Junkers joined Deutsche Continental Gasgesellschaft, who specialised in gas powered engines under the technical direction of Wilhelm von Oechelhäuser. Junkers already had experience of this form of power from his studies in Berlin.

## Early experiments in Dessau

Junkers now became immersed in attempting to solve and research any technical problem thrown at him and it was not long before he set up the first of many companies. In partnership with Oechelhauser, he formed a new experimental establishment at Dessau, 50 miles southwest of Potsdam in the heart of Germany. Named the Versuchsanstalt für Gasmotoren (Laboratory of Gas Engines) von Oechelhäuser und Junkers, the main aim of the new company was to produce an industrial engine which could circumvent the four-stroke cycle, as patented by Nicolaus August Otto. This same patent saw many engineers, including Karl Benz, working on the two-stroke cycle and eventually overcome all the problems associated with it. Financially backed with Oechelhäuser's money, Junkers successfully produced an opposed-piston, two-stroke engine which was capable of running on waste gas created from a low-energy blast furnace. The first major success for Junkers, his engine was in service in steelworks across Germany from 1896.

On October 31, 1893, Junkers formed his first company by the name of Hugo Junkers Civil-Ingenieur in Dessau, a decision prompted by his wish to patent all of the hard work he had put into producing the opposed-piston gas engine. Renamed Junkers und Compagnie (ICO) on July 1, 1895, the firm grew from strength to strength by specialising in the production of hot-water heaters, sheet metal ducting and ventilation equipment plus a host of patented designs including a calorie measuring device, which was clearly decades ahead of its time. Dr Robert Ludwig, who studied with Junkers during his time in Berlin, joined ICO to provide financial backing. However, within two years, a dispute over who was the majority shareholder saw Ludwig depart on July 1, 1897.

## Professor at Aachen

During this early period of ICO, Junkers never gave up trying to gain a technical position with a university in Germany. In September 1897 Professor Junkers was employed by the Technical High School of Aachen, where he taught thermodynamics and was allowed to carry out a large number of experiments in the school's laboratories.

**The great Professor Hugo Junkers, who was the son of a mill-owner, had created a giant network of engineering companies many years before he had even considered becoming involved in aviation. Ultimately, when austere economic times began to bite by the early 1930s, Junkers was only interested in saving his aviation and aircraft engine manufacturing businesses.**

Not long after his appointment at Aachen, Junkers at the age of 39 married 22-year-old Therese Bennhold on March 31, 1898, the daughter of Carl Bennhold who was headmaster of the Dessau High School. The couple went on to have no less than twelve children, the first; Herta was born in Aachen on January 9, 1899, a town where the Junkers family would live until 1920.

**The Hans Reissner-designed 'Ente' (Duck) canard pusher monoplane; the wings were constructed in the Junkers factory in Dessau. This is the aircraft in its original 'exposed-fuselage' form prior to its maiden flight in May 1912.**

## The aviation bug begins to bite

Early efforts by the growing number of aviation pioneers did not escape the attention of Hugo Junkers. Despite approaching the age of 50, Junkers became increasing interested in the subject, especially since the Wright brothers' first powered flight in 1903, and again when Hans Reissner arrived in Aachen to work as a professor in the school. Reissner was very interested in anything to do with aircraft, especially aerodynamics, to such a point he purchased a French Voisin biplane. Reissner spent a great deal of time dismantling and re-assembling the Voisin in several different ways, using a parade ground at Branderheided in Aachen to test his modifications. Junkers was always on hand to assist Reissner in his experiments; culminating in a very short flight, more like a 'hop', which took place at Branderheided on April 12, 1909. It was not long before the Voisin had served its purpose and in order to progress his ideas and theories, Reissner decided to design and build his own aircraft. Junkers was very excited about the idea and in 1910 Reissner began drawing the plans for the aircraft, which would be named the 'Ente' ('Duck').

Even with the very first aircraft Junkers was associated with, he suggested it could be made of metal when the rest of the world used wood and fabric. Reissner was obviously influenced by Junker's ideas because the fuselage of the 'Ente' was an open framework made of steel tubing. A canard design, the engine, a 70hp Argus, was mounted at the rear with a pair of rectangular shaped curved wings made from thin corrugated metal mounted in front. A pair of undercarriage wheels were mounted below each wing and at the front of the aircraft was mounted a fin and elevator with a third wheel underneath. The fuselage was built at the Research Institute in Aachen, while the wings were produced in Dessau due to the help of one of the Junkers' engineers. Reissner had already been awarded Patent No. 222 266, for his wing design, on November 5, 1908.

On May 23, 1912, the 'Ente' completed its successful maiden flight in the hands of one of Germany's earliest pilots Robert Gsell, who may have also demonstrated the aircraft at Johannisthal later in the

**Following the Duck's fatal crash in January 1913 the aircraft was rebuilt and flown again in the form depicted, complete with four large fins under the main plane and a fabric-covered fuselage.**

year. Unfortunately, the 'Ente' came to grief in Aachen when pilot Lucien Hild stalled the machine, killing himself and wrecking the aircraft on January 22, 1913. The stall was the most common killer of early pilots, a phenomenon that took a long while to understand.

Rebuilt in 1913, the 'Ente' re-emerged with an enclosed fabric-covered framework and four substantial fins were added to the underside of the main planes. It was at this point, the project now complete, that Junkers and Reissner went their separate ways.

Motivated by the 'Ente', Junkers threw himself into researching aerodynamics. He spent a great deal of time using the Technical High School's small wind tunnel, but to proceed with many of his ideas he would need a much bigger facility. In 1913 he had his own much larger Eiffel-type wind-tunnel, powered by a 100hp (74Kw) electric motor, constructed in nearby Frankenburg and another similar one built in Dessau. Junkers tested thousands of different model shapes in the tunnels, which yielded a plethora of results and information. One of the most significant results to come out of the wind tunnel testing for Junkers was the development of very thick wing sections which would prove to be both strong and aerodynamically efficient. Junkers also spent a lot of his time developing ideas of how to build aircraft out of sheet iron and later aluminium alloy.

## The Great War

Professor Junkers resigned from teaching when World War One broke out to focus on designing and building all-metal aircraft at Dessau. Plenty of funds were available for such an enterprise thanks to good sales of heaters and field kitchens for the German Army. By late 1915 a set of all-metal cantilever wings, with a steel tubular internal structure covered in a very thin sheet-iron surface were undergoing load-bearing tests. Not long after under the guidance of Professor Junkers the world's first all-metal aircraft, the Junkers J1, was designed by Otto Reuter and Otto Mader. Constructed in Dessau in September 1915 the J1 undertook its maiden flight on December 12, the first of many innovative aircraft to share the Junkers' name.



An early Lufthansa poster promoting the idea that a Junkers F13 could deliver you direct to the beach.

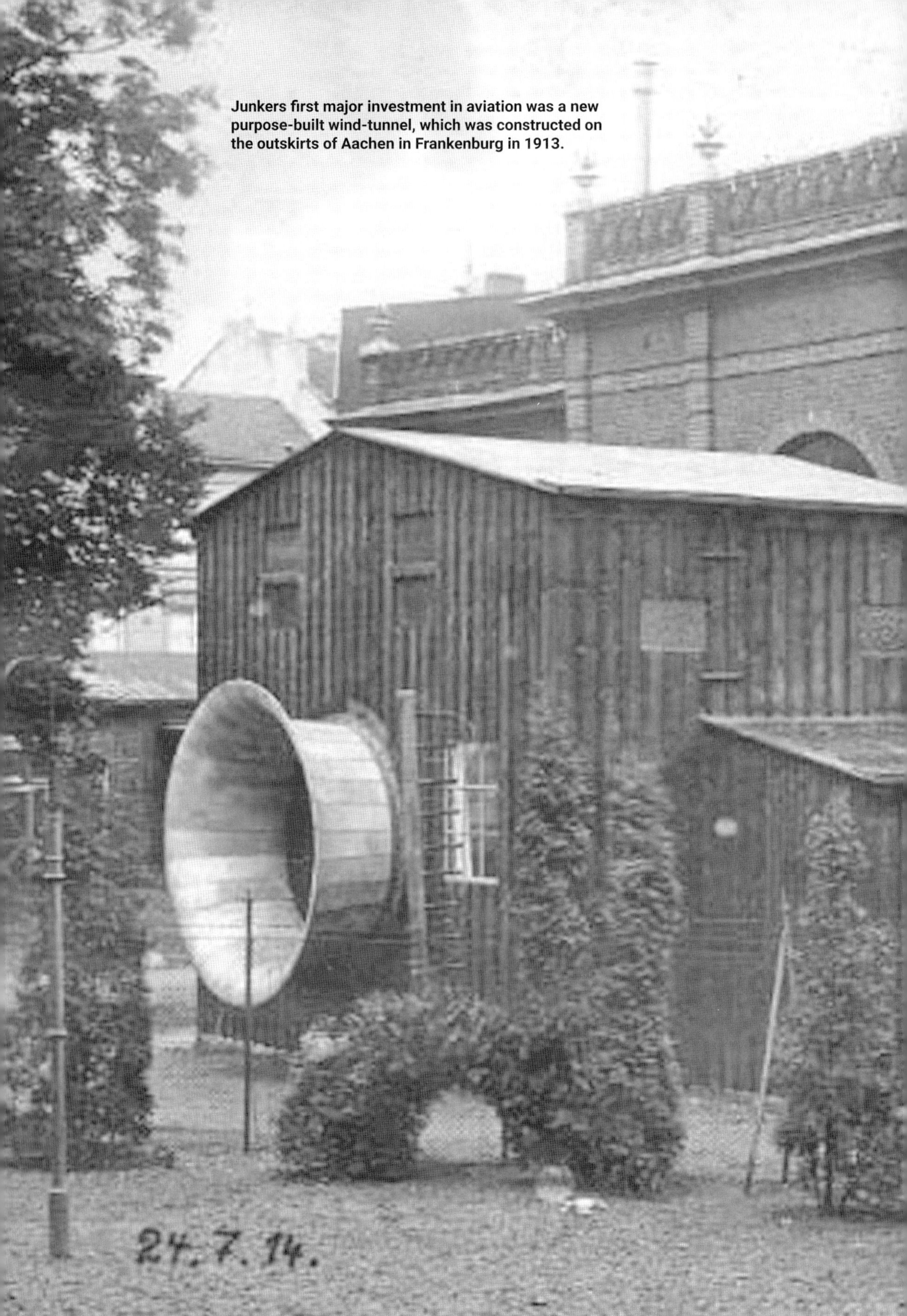

Junkers first major investment in aviation was a new purpose-built wind-tunnel, which was constructed on the outskirts of Aachen in Frankenburg in 1913.

2424
Archiv Bernd Junkers

In an attempt to improve the efficiency of military aircraft production during World War One the German Government decreed, on October 20, 1917, that Junkers and Fokker would work in partnership. The companies would become the Junkers-Fokker Flugzeugwerke A.G. located at Dessau. Hugo Junkers and Anthony Fokker never worked well together; the main purpose of the amalgamation was to use the proven Fokker production skills to mass produce the Junkers J4, J9, J10 and J11. Considerably less aircraft were produced than the German Government had hoped for and on April 24, 1919 Fokker departed, the company then being renamed Junkers Flugzeugwerke A.G.

## Beating the Allied restrictions

From 1919 onwards Junkers embarked on a large number of aircraft projects which started extremely well, particularly with the manufacture of the world's most influential airliner to date – the Junkers F13. At the same time, a new company airline was established under the name Junkers-Luftverkehr together with a new pilot training establishment called the Junkers Flugzeugführerschule (Pilot School). Moderately successful in its own right, Junkers-Luftverkehr was later merged with Deutscher Aero Lloyd (DAL) in 1926 which went on to form the national airline Deutsche Luft Hansa (from January 1, 1934 Deutsche Lufthansa).

The Junkers F13 was a huge success and a pioneering aircraft for all future airliners. Many were built in the Soviet factory in Fili, Moscow and several served the Russian airline Dobrolet.

## Engines and foreign ventures

In an attempt to keep every stage of the production of its airliners under the same roof, Junkers also began manufacturing its own aircraft engines with a new company called Junkers Motorenbau GmbH. As a result, the Junkers operation began to expand rapidly and its influence on the airlines began to be felt. Manufacturing licences to build Junkers aircraft outside Germany for the first time were issued, although this would lead to the first of several monetary disasters for the company.

Not long after the end of World War One the German and Soviet Governments entered into discussions about several different co-operative ventures. In hindsight this was an obvious attempt to get around the tight Allied restrictions that had been placed upon Germany with regard to the production of military aircraft and the training of military aircrew. In November 1922 permission was given for Junkers to develop a new factory at Fili in Moscow where Junkers aircraft would be built for the Soviet Air Force, supported with German money. This was followed in December 1923 by the Reichswehr-Ministerium (Reich Ministry) and the Soviet Government signing an agreement which allowed the training of German pilots at the Soviet airfield at Lipezk, east of Moscow.

Serious problems for Junkers began to arise when the German Government decided that they had lost interest in the whole idea and all financial aid was withdrawn. Government loans to Junkers were also ordered to be repaid forthwith. As a result, the company had virtually run out of money by October 1925 and was forced to sell two thirds of its shares to the German Government to secure further credit. The situation was so bad Hugo Junkers resigned; but he was back at the helm of the company by late 1926, when a repayment of 1 million Reichsmarks to the government was agreed. On top of this, Junkers were also ordered to supply 2.7 million Reichsmarks worth of aircraft to the government to clear old debts.

## The demise of Hugo Junkers

The next challenge that faced Junkers was the Great Depression of the early 1930s that would see many smaller companies fall by the wayside. Junkers managed to protect the aircraft and engine production parts of his empire by selling off the once profitable water heater and stationary engine companies. Even the arrival of the highly successful Ju 52 could not stop the money running out again, but the

**Otto Reuter joined Junkers as a technical designer in late 1915 and, before his premature death at the age of 36 in 1922, he was involved with the Junkers J1, J4, J7, F13, J15 and K16.**

Junkers' first aircraft to be produced in significant numbers was the Junkers J4 (J1 in German Air Force service). Nicknamed the armoured Furniture Van (Möbelwagen), nearly 300 were built with many seeing active service with the German Air Force right to the very end of World War One.

final death nail for Hugo Junkers was the arrival of Adolf Hitler and his Nazi party, which gained power on January 30, 1933.

In typical Nazi style, a series of false charges were issued against Hugo Junkers in order to put pressure on him to relinquish all of his patents and control of the companies based at Dessau. The Nazis had plans to mass produce military aircraft to rebuild the Luftwaffe and they knew that Hugo Junkers' main interest was civilian aircraft. By February 1934, Junkers was under open arrest in his home in Bayrischzell with strict orders to contact none of his companies. Sadly his health began to fail and on February 3, 1935, his 76th birthday, one of the world's great aviation pioneers passed away.

All of Junkers assets became State-owned following his demise and Dr Heinrich Koppenberg was appointed as Director General. On July 5, 1936 the aircraft and engine production companies were merged to become Junkers Flugzeug- und Motorenbau GmbH with Koppenberg as chairman. Suddenly, the colossal debt that Junkers had owed was gone and the company now had a capital of 130 million Reichsmarks; it could boast to being one of the biggest aircraft engine manufacturers in the world.

Hugo Junkers was never comfortable designing or building military aircraft but relished the opportunity to research and develop the subject. However, he wasted no time turning his attention back to his true passion – civilian air transport – once World War One came to an end. By the 1930s it was obvious that Germany was preparing for war again and once more Junkers was forced to do work he was not comfortable with. Junkers had achieved huge success in producing the world's first airliner, influencing the development of many new air transport routes across the globe together with an array of record-breaking flights. Junkers had also advanced aircraft construction methods, but the bottom line was that Hugo Junkers was not a businessman; his aircraft company was not a financial success, and its production output was not that impressive either. Admittedly, Junkers was often caught out by adverse political decisions, and no one could escape the Great Depression. However, first and foremost Hugo Junkers was an engineer who was more interested in the technical aspects of building aircraft rather than producing them in great numbers at a profit.

## Nazi control

All focus at Junkers was now on the design and development of single and twin-engined military aircraft as ordered by the Reichsluftfahrtministerium (RLM), although two civilian designs that broke that rule were the Ju 52 and the Ju 90. The former was already a popular aircraft with civilian airlines and by the beginning of World War Two, 400 were in service across the globe.

The long tradition of a corrugated surface was dispensed with when the Ju 86 appeared in 1934, an aircraft that was thinly veiled as a commercial airliner but was clearly more suited as a bomber. Similar in proportions at least was the four-engined Ju 89 which was developed under 'Ural bomber' programme, but Germany's future bomber force would not be centred on four-engined heavies, like the Allies. A spin-off from the Ju 89 was the Ju 90 which was designed to carry passengers over great distances including scheduled flights across the Atlantic. A protracted development, disrupted by the loss of two prototypes, did not see the aircraft gain certification until 1939, by which time the war was rapidly approaching and all Ju 90s were destined only to serve the Luftwaffe in either transport or long-range maritime reconnaissance roles.

One of the most iconic aircraft that achieved astonishing success for the Luftwaffe during the early stages of World War Two was the Ju 87 'Stuka'. Used effectively at the sharp end of Germany's Blitzkrieg strategy, the Ju 87 was employed as a tactical bomber which could be brought into use more quickly than long range artillery. After being withdrawn from this role, Junkers redesigned and rejuvenated the Ju 87 so that it could be employed in other theatres of war; one of the most successful was as a 'tank buster' against Soviet armour which continued right until the end of the conflict.

While the Ju 87 was good, it did not compare with one of the greatest multi-role combat aircraft of World War Two, the Ju 88. The mainstay light bomber of the Luftwaffe from its entry into service in 1939 the Ju 88 was also employed as a dive-bomber, night fighter and in the anti-shipping role. It would see action during the Polish Campaign, the Battle of Norway, Battle of France, Battle of Britain and on the Eastern Front. From 1943 it also served with the Finish Air Force which did not relinquish the type until 1948. A huge range of variants of the Ju 88 were manufactured, production finally ending with over 15,000 built. The Ju 88 spawned several other derivatives, none of which would ever replace it, including the Ju 188 and Ju 388.

Meanwhile the Ju 52 success story also continued, the military versions entering Luftwaffe service in 1934. The type remained the most highly used air transport aircraft in the Luftwaffe inventory and like the Ju 87 first cut its teeth in action, as a bomber, during the Spanish Civil War. Production

**The dream of a giant flying-wing capable of carrying fare-paying passengers across the globe almost came to fruition with the Junkers G38.**

One of the main disadvantages of building metal, rather than wooden aircraft was the amount of time the machine took to produce. However, Junkers was more interested in producing a beautifully crafted aircraft which could last for 20 years in all conditions with minimum maintenance. These are Junkers G24s under construction at Dessau during the late 1920s.

By the beginning of World War Two the Junkers Ju 52/3m provided the backbone to the Luftwaffe's transport capability and remained so until the end of the conflict. These aircraft, belonging to 1./KG 102, have just fallen into Norwegian hands at Hartvigvannet in May 1940.

The Ju 52/3m was a colossal success for the company, but Hugo Junkers was destined never to enjoy it. Produced in huge numbers, the influence of the Nazi party saw the military variants of this tri-engined airliner dramatically outnumber the civilian aircraft from 1934 onwards. Even those that appeared to be operated in civilian role – including D-2600 *Immelmann* shown here over Nuremburg – were in fact, very often, already in the hands of the Luftwaffe.

continued throughout the war, but even in 1939 the aircraft was obsolete. Like so many Junkers designs a potential replacement was never developed in time, so it was just easier to continue producing the original aircraft. As result, the Ju 52 took very high losses beginning in Holland with the so called 'Battle for The Hague' on May 10, 1940. 280 Ju 52s were lost during the large-scale aerial attack, many to accurate Dutch anti-aircraft guns while many more were wrecked landing at unsuitable airfields. Regardless, the Ju 52/3m will always remain both as Junkers' most successful commercial aircraft and its most prolific military air transport, which even remained in post-war production with CASA in Spain and A.A.C in France.

## A post-war survivor

Junkers aircraft production came to an abrupt end in late April 1945 with the arrival of US forces at Dessau, but by August what remained was in Soviet hands. Under the designation OKB-1, the Soviets established a small research and development team at Dessau while the Junkers' staff was allowed to continuing working on the Ju 287, EF 126 and EF 131 projects. This was the state of affairs until October 22, 1946 when the entire Junkers' operation was moved to Russia. Several developments of later Junkers' designs were worked on in Russia and new projects such as the EF 140 and EF 150 for the Soviet Air Force were undertaken. None of them came to fruition and from 1952 the Junkers operation in Russia was steadily reduced and the last German employees were repatriated in 1955.

**The first of approximately 6,500 Ju 87s built, with a 640hp Rolls-Royce Kestrel V engine as the intended Jumo 210 Inverted-Vee engine was not ready in time for the maiden flight. Junkers had already pioneered the dive bomber with the A48, the idea being rejuvenated by Ernst Udet during the early 1930s.**

Many returning ex-Junkers employees helped to create the new East German Aircraft Industry (Volkseigener Betriebe Flugzeugbau (VEB)) which was established at Klotsche near Dresden. The German Democratic Republic (GDR or East Germany) Government had initially planned to establish the country's new aviation industry at the original Junkers plant at Dessau. It was at Klotsche that Germany's first attempt at producing a jet-powered commercial airliner took place in the shape of the unattractive Baade BB 152. First flown by Willi Lehmann the 152, capable of carrying 72 passengers, took to the air on December 4, 1958. The aircraft was lost on only its second flight in March 1959 and by the time a second prototype flew jet-powered commercial airliners were already entering service. On April 5, 1961 the GDR Government closed the Klotsche establishment which in many people's eyes was the true end to the Junkers story as so many original employees had worked for the VEB.

In the new West Germany (the Federal Republic of Germany) a Junkers design centre was established in Munich under the original name, Junkers GmbH (ex-Junkers Flugzeugwerke) during the 1950s. However, Junkers GmbH was engaged in designing an orbital spacecraft, designated as the RT8, rather than traditional aircraft. The RT8, which was the brainchild of Eugen Sänger, was a reusable machine weighing 180 tons and capable of carrying a 2.8-ton payload. The orbiter was launched on the back of a 'mother ship' which was designed to release the RT8 into orbit. The 'mother ship' would return safely to earth while the RT8, code named 'Horus' (Hypersonic Orbital Upper Stage), continued on its journey. A great deal of the development work carried out on the RT8 was to prove useful for future reusable spacecraft.

In 1958, Junkers GmbH merged with MBB (Messerschmitt-Bölkow-Blohm) along with Heinkel and Messerschmitt. Merger later turned into absorption and in 1969 the great name of Junkers finally disappeared for good.

**First flown by Willi Lehmann in December 1958, the Baade BB 152 was the GDR's failed attempt to break into the potentially lucrative jet-powered airliner market.**

The Junkers factory and airfield at Dessau captured on film by a USAAF Spitfire PR XIT on May 30, 1944. The site was abandoned by Junkers following their forced moved to Russia in 1946 but has generally remained intact and, today, in the north western corner an excellent 'Technik Museum' dedicated to Hugo Junkers and his aircraft keeps the memory alive.

**Along with CASA of Spain, the French, who were building Ju 52/3ms for the Luftwaffe throughout World War Two, continued production until 1947, the aircraft being redesignated as the AAC-1 Toucan.**

# J1

## Development

Professor Hugo Junkers made one of the most impressive entries into aircraft production by building the J1. Nicknamed the 'Blechesel', which using the most polite translation means 'Tin Donkey', the aircraft paved the way for all-metal construction.

## Design

Designed by Otto Reuter and Otto Mader, under the close guidance of Hugo Junkers, the plan was to build the aircraft from light duralumin (an alloy made up of copper, manganese and magnesium), but manufacturers were not willing to part with the precious material. Undaunted, Junkers decided to use sheet iron, rolled out to a thickness of 0.1 to 0.2mm which would be used to skin the wing. To give the skin strength, which was made up of short hollow aerofoil sections, it was corrugated giving the surface a look that would remain with Junkers aircraft right through to the Ju 52.

The fuselage was built up of wooden formers with thin corrugated sheet wrapped around it. The wings were attached to fuselage via a host of bracing tubes and three connecting points. The tail was also all-metal, completed with a balanced rudder but no fixed fin. The sturdy looking machine also had a braced undercarriage and a tailskid, while power was provided by a 120hp Mercedes D.II water-cooled, six cylinder engine.

## Service

Work began on the J1 in September 1915, and considering the complexity of its construction, the aircraft was ready for its maiden flight by late November. On December 12, 1915 the world's first

all-metal aircraft took off from Doeberitz for its maiden flight in the hands of Lt Friedrich von Mallinkrodt. Although it was obvious the design of the aircraft was pitched at being a fighter, without armament the J1 showed promising performance at low-level compared with contemporary aircraft in service at the time. However, the J1s climb performance at 150ft/min was poor because of the weight of the all-metal construction; the Fokker E.III, weighed in at just 1,345lb against the J1's 2,270lb.

From the day the first J1 flew, which was destined to be the only example, all efforts were expended on making the aircraft lighter. This was never fully achieved, as more effort was placed on resolving an inherent structural weakness created by how the wings were fitted to the fuselage. The problem was exposed further in January 1916 when a wing cracked after a heavy landing. After repairs the aircraft was involved in further experimental flying until March.

The J1 had given Junkers a great deal of experience in a very short time, the entire project lasting a mere four months from first to last flight. The J1 was preserved and later exhibited at the Junkers Lehrhaus (Junkers Educational Exhibit) at Dessau, before being moved to the Deutsches Museum in Munich. Sadly, this pioneering little aircraft was destroyed by Allied bombing during World War Two.

| Technical Data – Junkers J1 | |
| --- | --- |
| ENGINE | One 120hp Mercedes D.II |
| WINGSPAN | 42ft 5in |
| LENGTH | 28ft 3½in |
| WING AREA | 258sq ft |
| LOADED WEIGHT | 2,270lb |
| MAX SPEED | 106mph |
| CLIMB RATE | 150ft/min |

**Lt Friedrich von Mallinkrodt (on loan from the IdFlieg – the Inspectorate of Flying Troops) warms through the Junkers J1s 120hp Mercedes D.III engine at Doeberitz prior to the aircraft undertaking its maiden flight on December 12, 1915.**

# J2

## Development

The pioneering work and thought that had gone into the J1 had not escaped the attention of Hauptmann Felix Wagenführ, the head of the IdFlieg's Prüfanstalt und Werft der Fliegertruppe (Test Establishment and Workshop of the Aviation Troops). A contract was issued to Junkers for six all-metal fighter monoplane prototypes, powered by the same Mercedes engine as the J1 and armed with a single 7.92mm Spandau synchronised machine gun.

## Design

Designed by Otto Mader, the J2 differed from the earlier aircraft in many ways; one being the way the wing was attached to the fuselage by moving it forward of the cockpit. This allowed for a wing centre section that was integrated into the fuselage structure, with the outer wing sections attached via four threads.

The fighter was very streamlined; the Mercedes D.II, driving a two-bladed propeller, was completely enclosed. The fuselage was covered in a thin metal skin without a hint of external bracing, only disrupted by a roll bar behind the cockpit to protect the pilot. The undercarriage struts were thin, offering very little wind resistance while engine cooling was solved by mounting the radiator, directly below the cockpit, in a fashion reminiscent of a particularly famous Allied fighter of World War Two.

## Service

The first J2, the world's first all-metal fighter, serialled E 250/16 made its maiden flight on July 11, 1916 from Doeberitz in the hands of Lt Mallinkrodt. From the outset, it was clear the J2 would need numerous modifications, which began with a more powerful engine – the 160hp Mercedes D.III. Other alterations included an increase in span of 2ft 3in, a shorter chord, which reduced the area by 13 sq/in, longer span ailerons and a marginal increase in the length of the fuselage. Subsequent aircraft incorporated all of these modifications as well as, from the third aircraft, a new rudder which had a leading edge shaped like a semi-circle.

Nine miles per hour faster than all of its contemporaries the J2 exuded very good handling characteristics but was, once again, let down by a poor climb rate while visibility from the cockpit was not the best. As a result, no further orders were received; a decision rubber stamped when the second prototype, E 251/16, crashed on September 23, 1916, killing the pilot, Max Schade.

## Production

Six confirmed J2s built for the IdFlieg contract, serialled E 250/16 to E255/16, but it is possible that Junkers also built a seventh or even eighth example.

| Technical Data – Junkers J2 | |
| --- | --- |
| ENGINE | (Prototype) One 120hp Mercedes D.II; one 160hp Mercedes D.III |
| WINGSPAN | 38ft 6½in |
| LENGTH | 24ft 5½in |
| HEIGHT | 10ft 3in |
| WING AREA | 265sq ft |
| EMPTY WEIGHT | 2,249lb |
| LOADED WEIGHT | 2,569lb |
| MAX SPEED | 115mph |
| CLIMB RATE | 9,840ft in 21 minutes |
| RANGE | 149 miles |
| ARMAMENT | One 7.92mm Spandau IMG 08/15 machine gun |

The second of just three J2s built to a IdFlieg contract submitted in January 1916 was E 252/16.

# J4

## Development

There was no doubt that the designs and ideas of Junkers were making an impression on the German military, but the all-metal aircraft were not ideal as fighters. They could be more usefully employed as ground attack aircraft, where their metal frames would provide protection to the crew from small arms fire as they flew contact patrol duties, flying dangerously low over the trenches.

## Design

The new aircraft, designated the J4, was designed by Otto Reuter, engineers Steudal and Brandenburg and Professor Dr G Madelung who, from the mid-1930s, worked on designs for flying bombs. All of the main ideas used in the J3 were employed in the J4, the aircraft having a Duralumin fuselage of tubular construction and wings made of Duralumin sheets and tubes.

The 200hp Benz Bz IV six-cylinder in-line powerplant was, along with the two-man crew, encased in an armoured chrome-nickel steel tunnel to protect the occupants and the engine from ground fire. A more powerful 256hp Mercedes D IVa was trialled in one aircraft giving it a better rate of climb, but the manufacturer, Daimler, could not match the potential demand for the engine.

## Service

The first of three prototypes, serialled 425/17, completed its maiden flight on January 28, 1917. Production began in June following an order for 50 aircraft, the first of them entering service from August 1917 over the front-line trenches.

The J4, known as the J.1 in military service, was by far the most successful Junkers aircraft of World War One from a production and service point of view. The heavy biplane needed a longer than average runway to become airborne, but once the aircraft was in the air it certainly looked after its crews. Not only was the aircraft reliable but the steel tunnel which encased the crew afforded a great deal of protection, and at least one J4 returned home with 400 small-arms' hits.

The J4 served the German Air Force right to the end of World War One and production continued into the post-war period. During this time it is believed that several J4s were transferred to the Austrian Air Force.

## Production

Production of the J4 reached 227, in several batches, that stemmed from original orders totalling 283 aircraft. This was made up of three prototypes, 425 to 427/17, followed by five production batches constructed from late 1917 through to early 1919. 184 aircraft were delivered to the IdFlieg by October 1918 and a further 43 were completed in peacetime.

| Technical Data – Junkers J4 | |
|---|---|
| **ENGINE** | One 200hp Benz Bz IV |
| **WINGSPAN** | (Upper) 52ft 6in; (Lower) 35ft 7in |
| **LENGTH** | 29ft 10¼in |
| **HEIGHT** | 11ft 1¾in |
| **WING AREA** | 533sq ft |
| **EMPTY WEIGHT** | 3,892lb |
| **LOADED WEIGHT** | 4,798lb |
| **MAX SPEED** | 96mph |
| **CLIMB RATE** | 9,840ft in 21 minutes |
| **RANGE** | 192 miles |
| **ARMAMENT** | Two fixed, forward-firing, 7.92mm LMG 08/15 machine guns and one 7.92mm Parabellum in the rear cockpit |

*Right*: **The prototype J4, 425/17, pictured on May 23, 1917. The sturdy looking biplane was nicknamed the 'Furniture Van' by pilots who were used to flying more nimble machines.**

*Below*: **Only two J4s survive today, one can be seen in the Technikmuseum in Berlin while the other is currently in store at the National Aeronautical Collection of Canada at Rockcliffe. The latter, serialled 518/18, is pictured here not long after it fell into Allied hands. The aircraft was shipped to Canada in 1919 before going into storage with the RCAF.**

# J7

## Development

Junkers, Mader and Reuter set about designing another new fighter in July 1917, designated as the J7. The project started as an 'experimental venture' with the support of the IdFlieg. The aircraft was based on the J3, plus ideas created by the stillborn J5 and J6.

## Design

Short and stubby in appearance, Junkers' latest little fighter was the world's first all-Duralumin, low-wing monoplane. The majority of the structure was covered in corrugated Duralumin skin over the top of a Duralumin tubular frame. The wing was made up of seven tubular aluminium spars interconnected by a 'Warren Girder' frame work and was fitted with unequal chord un-balanced ailerons. The aircraft first appeared with novel rotating wing tips for roll control, before these were replaced by more conventional ailerons. The vertical fin, pivoted at its central point, acted as a rudder, while the elevators were horn-balanced.

The undercarriage was a very sturdy braced design, as was the tail skid. Power was provided by a water-cooled Mercedes D.IIIa engine with the radiator mounted on top of the forward fuselage. The radiator was later moved to a more aerodynamic position in front of the cowling. A substantial fairing behind the cockpit enclosed a crash pylon.

## Service

First flown on September 17, 1917, by Arved von Schmidt, several modifications were made to the fighter in preparation for its entry into a competition to select a new biplane fighter for the German Air Force, at Adlershof in February 1918. The modifications included changes to the undercarriage, removal of a spinner and the fairing behind the cockpit was taken off to reveal the bare pylon.

Prior to the Adlershof competition the J7 was seriously damaged in an accident with Anthony Fokker at the controls, but the aircraft was repaired before the contest. At first, because the J7 was a monoplane, the aircraft was not allowed to enter the competition, but once the performance of the fighter was revealed the rules were relaxed. After testing by IdFlieg, three further aircraft were ordered in March 1918. Larger orders were held back until Junkers could improve its production facilities, which had suffered many delays during the manufacture of the J4.

However, within a short period of time the development of the J9 had already overtaken the J7 and the order for three further machines, which were already partially built, was transferred to the new aircraft. Only one J7 reached flight stage but no military serial was applied, the aircraft being allocated Junkers construction number J0303.

| Technical Data – Junkers J7 | |
|---|---|
| ENGINE | One 120hp Mercedes D.IIIa |
| WINGSPAN | 30ft 2¼in |
| LENGTH | 22ft |
| HEIGHT | 8ft 6¼in |
| WING AREA | 126sq ft |
| EMPTY WEIGHT | 1,446lb |
| LOADED WEIGHT | 1,841lb |
| MAX SPEED | 149mph |
| CLIMB RATE | 16,400ft in 23.7 minutes |
| CEILING | 19,680ft |

The one and only Junkers J7 after modifications had been applied prior to the aircraft's entry into the Adlershof fighter selection competition.

# J8 (CL)

## Development

Unconvinced that the biplane was the way forward, Junkers was adamant that a cantilever monoplane design could deliver better performance. To prove this point, a military version of the J7 brought about the J8.

## Design

Officially designated as the CL, the J8 was an all-metal, Duralumin corrugated-skin, close-support aircraft. Similar in appearance to the J7, the fuselage was longer to accommodate both the pilot and an observer, the latter being equipped with a single machine gun for self-defence. The wingspan was increased to improve low speed handling, and roll control benefited from larger ailerons which extended beyond the wing tip.

The J8 was powered by an upright 160hp Mercedes D.IIIa six-cylinder, water-cooled, in-line engine, driving a twin bladed propeller.

## Service

IdFlieg placed an order for three J8s on December 26, 1916, but owing to the distraction of J4 production the prototype was not ready for its first flight until December 10, 1917. The prototype J8 was first demonstrated to IdFlieg in February 1918 which designated the aircraft as Junk CL, and as a test machine it was serialled 'J8I'. Following the prototype's demonstration the IdFlieg requested further development of the aircraft, which would lead to the J10. However in the meantime, Junkers had entered into a joint-venture with Anthony Fokker resulting in the Junkers-Fokker Werke A.G. Fokker

This is the first of just four J8 (CL) close-support aircraft built by Junkers in late 1917, shown here on January 2, 1918.

was very interested in producing the J8 as was IdFlieg, but it was not convinced that the newly formed partnership was up to the job.

Two further J8 prototypes, 'J8II' and 'J8III' were both in the air by May 1918, followed by a fourth aircraft, which was used by Junkers for general development and flight testing.

## Production

Four J8s in total were built, 'J8I' (J0307), 'J8II' (J0308) first flown on March 18, 1918, and used for structural testing at Adlershof, 'J8III' (J0309) first flown on May 18, 1918, and 'J8' (J0310) which was used solely for experimental flying.

| Technical Data – Junkers J8 | |
|---|---|
| ENGINE | One 160hp Mercedes D.IIIA |
| WINGSPAN | 40ft |
| LENGTH | 25ft 11in |
| HEIGHT | 10ft 2in |
| WING AREA | 291sq ft |
| EMPTY WEIGHT | 1,621lb |
| LOADED WEIGHT | 2,547lb |
| MAX SPEED | 118mph |
| CRUISING SPEED | 96mph |
| CLIMB RATE | 3,280ft in 3.9 minutes |
| ENDURANCE | 2 hours |

# J9 (D1)

## Development

A development of the J7, the J9 – designated by the military as the D1 – was a late entrant into World War One. The J7 had left a good impression and as result, three developed versions were ordered by the IdFlieg in 1917.

## Design

Compared to the J7, Junkers' latest fighter had broader, shorter span wings. The engine installation was much neater and more powerful, giving the aircraft an impressive top speed of 150mph. Power, in the production aircraft, was provided by a 160hp Mercedes D.III engine, although two experimental versions were trialled with a 185hp BMW IIIa and a185hp Benz Bz IIIbm; the latter aircraft being designated as a J9B.

The J9 was covered in an all-corrugated skin and the undercarriage was much longer compared to the J7. Armament was a pair of synchronised fixed Spandau machine guns mounted on top of the forward fuselage.

## Service

The first J9 (J0311), serialled 2266/18, was flown in April 1918, and not long after a production order for ten aircraft was placed; the aircraft to be built at Dessau.

During May and June 1918, the prototype J9 was entered into the regular fighter contest, held at Adlershof. The J9 was compared to the Fokker DVII, already in production, and while the Junkers fighter had high speed and manoeuvrability in its favour, the aircraft was very difficult to build. As a result the aircraft was seen to be of more use in a balloon-busting role, rather than a fighter.

More aircraft were ordered, but none of them were in German service prior to November 1918, although several did see action immediately after World War One. The J9, alongside the J10, saw action with the Geschwader Sachsenburg in Finland, Estonia and Lithuania, in fighting against the Bolshevik forces. One J9, 5929/18, was captured by the Allies, or more likely was acquired in peacetime, and briefly used by the French Air Force during 1919. This aircraft is the only survivor and is on display in the Musée de l'Air at Le Bourget.

A few J9s were fitted with Duralumin floats after the war, the first such Junkers design to be so equipped. A least one J9 was entered, and was well-placed, in the Tyrrhenian Cup at Naples in 1922.

## Production

In total, 41 J9s (D1) were built, including the prototype 2266/18. The remainder were built in batches of ten beginning with 3110/18 to 3119/18 and 5170/18 to 5179/18; both of these batches were delivered in March 1919. 5180/18 to 5189/18 were part of an experimental production line and were delivered in November 1918 and 9160/18 to 9169/18 were delivered in March 1919. A further batch of 20 J9s was cancelled.

| Technical Data – Junkers J9 & J9B | |
|---|---|
| ENGINE | One 160hp Mercedes D.IIIA; one 185hp BMW IIIa; (J9B) one 185hp Benz Bz IIIbm |
| WINGSPAN | 29ft 6¼in |
| LENGTH | 23ft 9½in |
| HEIGHT | 8ft 6¼in |
| WING AREA | 159sq ft |
| EMPTY WEIGHT | 1,442lb |
| LOADED WEIGHT | 1,839lb |
| MAX SPEED | 140mph |
| CLIMB RATE | 16,400ft in 24 minutes |
| ENDURANCE | 1½ hours |
| ARMAMENT | Two fixed Spandau 7.9mm LMG 08/15 machine guns |

*Above*: A tidy looking fighter, the J9, here displaying its military designation D1 along the fuselage, only entered limited production at the very end of World War One.

*Right*: The very neat installation of the J9s Mercedes D.III engine is shown off to great effect, as is the all-corrugated Duralumin skin.

# J10 (CL1)

## Development

Following the successful demonstration carried out by the J8 at Adlershof in February 1918, a contract was won by Junkers for a modified version of the two-seat close support aircraft, designated as the J10, or CL1 in military service.

## Design

An extension of both the J7 and J9 series of aircraft, the prototype J10 made its maiden flight on May 4, 1918. Once again, the now hallmark, Junkers corrugated Duralumin skin was employed throughout the airframe, as was the tubular metal framework within it. The fuselage was a square frame with a rounded, raised coaming fitted to the upper surface. Once again, the strength of the airframe was far superior to any other aircraft of the day.

Powered by a Mercedes D.III, the J10 would cruise comfortably at 100mph on the engines 160hp. The aircraft's straight wings had squared off tips with flush-fitting ailerons while the rudder/fin and elevator was a single section.

The observer's cockpit was deliberately set behind the wing to afford him excellent visibility and a good field of fire for his single Parabellum machine gun. The pilot had a pair of forward-fixed Spandau machine guns in the same position as the J9. Along each side of the fuselage the aircraft had racks for signal cartridges.

## Service

The first half-dozen J10s were delivered in October 1918, too late for operational service with the German Air Force but time enough to evaluate the type for future use. Like the J9, the type did see limited action with the Geschwader Sachsenberg during fighting against the Bolsheviks in the Baltic region and, at least one example is known to have served with the Latvian Air Force.

Two aircraft, later registered as D-77 and D-78 were converted into passenger carrying aircraft by replacing the observer's position with an enclosed cabin. These aircraft first appeared in early 1919 and from March were operated by the Junkers-Luftverkehr (Junkers-Aviation) on a 70-mile route between Weimar and Dessau. This is believed to be the first occasion when an all-metal aircraft was used for commercial operations. D-78 later appeared on the civilian registry as being owned and operated by Lloyd-Luftverkehrs Sablatnig.

## Production

There were 43 J10s built from June 1918 to early March 1919, including one prototype serialled 1800/18 (J0373). Exact range of production aircraft serials is unclear, but they were between 1801/18 to 1863/18. Two batches of 20 and ten aircraft ordered in October 1918 were later cancelled.

| Technical Data – Junkers J10 | |
| --- | --- |
| ENGINE | One 160hp Mercedes D.IIIA; one 185hp BMW IIIa |
| WINGSPAN | 40ft |
| LENGTH | 25ft 11in |
| HEIGHT | 10ft 2in |
| WING AREA | 291sq ft |
| EMPTY WEIGHT | 1,621lb |
| LOADED WEIGHT | 2,547lb |
| MAX SPEED | 118mph |
| CRUISING SPEED | 96mph |
| CLIMB RATE | 3,280ft in 3.9 minutes |
| ENDURANCE | 2 hours |

*Right*: Junkers J10 (CL1), 1802/18 (J0375), the third of the type built, pictured resplendent in camouflage and iron crosses during initial evaluation by the German Air Force.

*Below*: Pictured on March 24, 1919, this is D-77, the first of two J10s converted to carry a single passenger in an enclosed cabin once occupied by the observer. The aircraft became the world's first all-metal commercial aircraft when it began flying a route between Weimar and Dessau.

# J11 (CLS1)

## Development

During early 1918 Junkers began putting forward the first of a series of proposals to the German Navy beginning with a variant of the J10, which could operate in a naval reconnaissance role. One option was a biplane version of the J10 while another, much preferred by Junkers, was a cantilever monoplane. Clearly swayed by Junkers the German Navy placed an order for three aircraft, designated by Junkers as the J11 and by the military as the CLS1.

## Design

Two J10s (7501 and 7503) were taken from the production line for conversion to J11 standard. Modifications included a new rear fuselage and a larger wing area, while a triangular-shaped fin – for increased stability – was fitted in front of the rudder. A pair of heavily braced floats was also attached.

The J11 was armed with a pair of fixed, forward-firing synchronised machine guns which were fitted directly in front of the cockpit on either side of the Benz Bz IIIa engine. A third machine gun was mounted on a swivel for the observer.

## Service

The first J11, 7501/18 (c/n J0433), completed its maiden flight in the hands of German Navy pilot Richard Thiedemann* on October 23, 1918. Two further aircraft, 7502/18 (c/n J0434) and 7503/18 (c/n J0435) were airborne not long after, but little is known about how well the aircraft handled because of the imminent end of World War One. As a result, the German Navy did not proceed with a large order, but flight trials of the J11 did continue in peace time and the information gleaned from the aircraft was later used for the floatplane variants of the A20 and F13.

---

* It was quite a fortuitous event for Richard Thiedemann to be sent to Dessau in 1918 to fly the J11, because it was to be the beginning of a long career with Junkers. By November 1919 Thiedemann was taken on as chief test pilot for Junkers Flugzeugwerke and not long after he was also appointed as the operational director. His rise continued when in 1924 he was promoted to technical director of IFA, and in 1937 he was appointed as the facility manager of Junkers Flugzeug and Motorenwerke AG. He remained in the latter position until 1945, but his association with aviation did not end there as he went on to become a director of Henschel Flugzeugwerke AG based in Kessel.

| Technical Data – Junkers J11 | |
| --- | --- |
| **ENGINE** | One 180hp Benz Bz IIIa |
| **WINGSPAN** | 41ft 10in |
| **LENGTH** | 28ft 10½in |
| **HEIGHT** | 10ft |
| **WING AREA** | 286sq ft |
| **EMPTY WEIGHT** | 2,018lb |
| **LOADED WEIGHT** | 3,131lb |
| **MAX SPEED** | 112mph |
| **CEILING** | 17,000ft |
| **RANGE** | 310 miles |
| **ARMAMENT** | Three machine guns, two fixed forward and one in the rear cockpit |

*Above*: The first of just three J11s built, at Dessau in October 1918. The aircraft has 'Junk. C.' stencilled on the side prior to its full military designation of CLS1 being applied.

*Right*: A good view of the re-designed tail surfaces of the J11, which now includes a more traditional fin to help improve stability.

# J13 (F13)

## Development

The forerunner of all specifically designed commercial transport aircraft the J13, commercial designation F13 (the F = Flugzeug), was also the first all-metal airliner. Aircraft were plentiful after World War One and many were ripe for conversion to civilian operations, however, Junkers were well aware that a purpose-built machine was needed to achieve commercial success.

## Design

Designed by Otto Reuter the F13, despite being a small aircraft, was way ahead of its time with regard to its structure and aerodynamics, and development would remain at the forefront of commercial aircraft design for the next twelve years.

Built entirely of Duralumin, the F13 could be easily dismantled for overseas customers. A fully enclosed cabin accommodated four passengers, complete with seatbelts, while the two-man crew occupied a semi-enclosed cockpit although this evolved into a fully enclosed version. The low wing was a thick cantilever design made up of nine duralumin spars strengthened with traverse bracing and covered by the traditional corrugated, stressed, duralumin skin.

Power for the early aircraft was provided by a Mercedes unit, but as the type evolved Junkers, Bristol and Jaguar engines were also employed, the latter producing 560hp compared to the first powerplants which could only muster just over 150hp.

## Service

The first aircraft, named after Hugo Junkers daughter Annelise, was first flown by company pilot Emil Monz on June 25, 1919. Regardless of the post-war restrictions being applied to Germany and the large number of surplus aircraft available from the war, the F13 began picking up orders from Austria, Poland and the United States from late 1919 onwards. In the US, John Larsen Aircraft bought a production licence for 28 aircraft which served with the US Navy, US Army Air Service, Mercury Airlines, Detroit-Chicago Airline and TNCA of Mexico as the JL-6.

By 1922, sales were spreading across Europe with aircraft being sold in Britain, France and Italy; while 60 F13s were flying in Germany alone by 1923 encouraged by the formation of Junkers own airline, Junkers Luftverkehr AG in 1921. Many aircraft were offered on a low-cost lease or even presented as gifts to encourage the fledgling airline industry to grow to a peak where 16 different operators were using the F13 across Europe. Junkers Luftverkehr was absorbed by Lufthansa in 1926, the latter operating 55 F13s at its peak across 43 routes until the type was retired in 1938.

Many F13s also saw military service with the Chinese, Columbian, Luftwaffe, Soviet and Turkish Air Forces through to the early 1930s.

## Production

In total, 322 F13s were built between 1923 and 1932 (the bulk of them by 1925) at Dessau and Fili (however, in Germany between 1921 and 1923 production was transferred to Danzig and Reval); 28 of this batch were reassembled by John Larsen Aircraft and redesignated as the JL-6.

| Technical Data – Junkers F 13 & A, Fe, Kae, Kao & Kay | |
|---|---|
| ENGINE | (13 & a) One 158hp Mercedes; (fe) one 305hp Junkers L5; (kae) one 475hp Jupiter IV; (kao) one 425hp Jaguar; (kay) one 560hp Jaguar Major |
| WINGSPAN | (13) 48ft 6¾in; (a to kay) 58ft 3in |
| LENGTH | (13 to fe) 31ft 6in; (kae to kay) 34ft 5½ in |
| HEIGHT | 11ft 10in |
| WING AREA | (13) 371sq ft; (a & fe) 463sq ft; (kae to kay) 484sq ft |
| EMPTY WEIGHT | (13) 2,095lb; (a) 2,558lb; (fe) 2,997lb; (kae) 3,142lb; (kao) 3,153lb; (kay) 3,319lb |
| LOADED WEIGHT | (13) 3,616lb; (a) 4,002lb; (fe) 5,072lb; (kae & kao) 5,954lb; (kay) 6,615lb |
| MAX SPEED | (13 & a) 106mph; (fe) 121mph; (kae) 130mph; (kao) 126mph; (kay) 143mph |
| CEILING | (kao) 16,400ft |
| RANGE | (13) 870 miles; (a) 745 miles; (fe) 578 miles; (kae) 326 miles; (kao) 357 miles; (kay) 323 miles |
| ACCOMMODATION | Two crew and four passengers |

*Right*: First flown in 1924, D-366 *Eismöwe* had a busy career with Junkers Luft Luftverkehrs AG, Lufthansa, Deruluft and RLM when it was re-registered as D-OHIL. The aircraft was recovered from Kabul in 1966 and is depicted after a long restoration, which was concluded in the late 1970s.

*Below*: Over 20 F13s were operated by the Austrian airline Ölag, including A-57 (c/n 593), which was christened *Dohle*.

# J15

## Development

Following the completion of the design work on the F13, a proposal was put forward for a three-seat passenger aircraft in August 1919. To carry through the ideas effectively Junkers built an experimental aircraft, designated as the J15, which could be configured either as a low- or high-wing monoplane.

## Design

The all-Duralumin built J15 was designed to carry two passengers in an enclosed cabin with a single pilot accommodated in an open cockpit set well back in the fuselage, behind the trailing edge of the wing.

Designed by Otto Mader, the J15 also benefitted from a great deal of input from aerodynamicist Phillip von Doepp. He was responsible for the wind tunnel at the Professor Junkers Research Institute, and it was his tests that indicated a high-wing configuration was better than a low position well before the aircraft took to the air.

However, the J15 was cleverly designed so that both wing configurations could be fitted; the low-wing connecting in the traditional manner and the high in a parasol arrangement. When the latter was employed the low-wing joints and profile were blanked off. Power was provided by a single upright, in-line Mercedes IIIa engine driving a four-bladed wooden propeller. The main undercarriage was mounted on pair of V-shaped legs, which were linked by axles that were braced by two struts on the centre line.

The one, and only, J15 with its wing in the high position. The tubby looking aircraft proved to be a very useful experimental machine, which paved the way for the successful J16 (K16) series of small airliners. Note the blanked off low-wing position.

## Service

The sole J15 (c/n 525) was ready for its maiden flight in September 1920, but to avoid unwarranted attention from the Allied inspection teams the aircraft was dismantled and moved by road to Holland. The exact location of the J15's first flight is unknown, but it was conducted on January 25, 1921, by Junkers test pilot, Wilhelm Zimmermann. The first flight took place initially with the wings in the low position and then the high/parasol position; the latter, as already suggested by Van Doepp, proved to be the better more stable configuration.

The J15 proved that a production version, to be designated the J16 (K16), was a definite proposition.

| Technical Data – Junkers J15 | |
|---|---|
| ENGINE | One 158hp Mercedes IIIa |
| WINGSPAN | 36ft 1in |
| LENGTH | 26ft 3in |
| WING AREA | 183sq ft |
| EMPTY WEIGHT | 948lb |
| LOADED WEIGHT | 1,570lb |
| MAX SPEED | 90mph |
| RANGE | 435 miles |
| ACCOMMODATION | One crew and two passengers |

# J16 (K16)

## Development

A slightly more compact version of the J15, the J16 (K16) – the 'K' standing for Kabinenflugzeug (cabin aircraft) – was a small general purpose transport aircraft capable of carrying two passengers. It was hoped that the J16 could be used on routes that the 'in service' F13 had yet to fully exploit, but the rapidly growing airline industry wanted aircraft that were bigger to take advantage of the more lucrative longer routes, so the majority of J16s ended up in private hands.

## Design

The J15 had exposed several design weaknesses, the most significant being the position of the pilot's cockpit which suffered from poor visibility. This was solved in the J16 by moving it in front of the leading edge of the wing, directly behind the engine. The open cockpit gave the pilot an outstanding field of view, which was crucial in the days when the only form of navigation was dead reckoning and being able to clearly see the ground and all of its features was vital. Both passengers were accommodated in an enclosed cabin directly below the high wing.

Power would prove to be a problem for the J16 because of Allied restrictions; the proposed 158hp Mercedes IIIa had to make way for the much less powerful 62hp Siemens Halske Sh4 radial. Power would be steadily increased as the aircraft evolved; the K16ba was fitted with the 80hp Sh4, the K16bi the Sh20, the K16bo a Walter NZ120 and finally the K16ce was powered by a 123hp Sh12 (Bristol Lucifer).

## Service

The J16/K16 prototype, D-390 (c/n 526) named *Trappe*, undertook its maiden flight in the hands of Wilhelm Zimmerman from Dessau on March 3, 1921. The same month, the Allied inspectors were making a concerted effort to fully restrict the German aircraft industry, so to prevent the K16 from being scrapped it was flown to Holland, where, along with the J15, it was secretly stored by Fokker until 1923. In July of that year the aircraft was seen in public in Gothenburg, returning to Dessau in early 1924 where several modifications were carried out. The same year Junkers began promoting the K16 to German airlines which tentatively experimented with the aircraft but were much more interested in larger passenger-carrying aircraft. As a result production was limited but the type did see some service with Lufthansa, Weimar Engineering College, Junkers Luftverkehr, Luftfrako, Deutraluft, Flughof G.m.b.H and Stormbird ('Sturmuogel') Flying Association. The latter, based at Berlin-Templehof, used a pair of K16s for joy-riding flights until 1933.

## Production

There were 17 J16/K16s built, all of them in 1925 at Dessau. Construction numbers were from 465 to 475 and 525 to 527, c/n 526 being the prototype named *Trappe*, which was later rebuilt as a K16a in April 1924.

| Technical Data – Junkers K16BA | |
|---|---|
| ENGINE | One 123hp Siemens Halske Sh 12 |
| WINGSPAN | 44ft |
| LENGTH | 26ft 3in |
| WING AREA | 205sq ft |
| EMPTY WEIGHT | 1,180lb |
| LOADED WEIGHT | 1,874lb |
| MAX SPEED | 106mph |
| CEILING | 13,100ft |
| RANGE | 373 miles |
| ACCOMMODATION | One crew and two passengers |

The prototype J16/K16 on the day of its maiden flight on March 3, 1921. Serialled D-390, the aircraft was named *Trappe* and, not long after this photo was taken, the aircraft was flown out of Germany to be stored in Holland away from Allied inspectors.

# J20 (A20, 25 and 35/K53)

## Development

In late 1922 Junkers and the Soviet Government joined forces to begin the construction of a new aircraft factory at Fili on the outskirts of Moscow. Not only would Fili be used for manufacturing, but also it would serve as a large maintenance hub for the bulk of the aircraft serving in the Soviet Air Force, which Junkers was hoping would predominantly be their own. The first aircraft to be built at Fili would be a new general-purpose machine designed by Mader and Zindel, based upon the J11 seaplane.

## Design

Designated as the J20 (later A20), the aircraft was a two-seat monoplane powered by a single 158hp Mercedes D.III engine. Constructed of corrugated Duralumin, the J20 was intended to be used for training and general military operations and/or as a mailplane.

Various versions for the A20 were set to follow, including the A20W (W-Water/floats), A20a powered by a 260hp Junkers L2, A20Be fitted with a 295hp BMW IV and the A20b powered by a 305hp L5 power plant. Once Allied restrictions were lifted in 1926 several A20s were converted to A25 standard which were fitted with the more powerful L2 engine, while the A35b and A35be used the L5.

One A20, D-361 'Sirius', was despatched to AB Flygindustri at Limhamn where the aircraft was transformed into a fighting machine complete with a single machine gun in the rear cockpit. No sales interest was generated by the aircraft which was designated as the R02. Re-engined with the L5, the aircraft was redesignated again in 1926 as the AFI R41. Sales success was achieved when an A35, fitted with the more purposeful L5 powerplant, was converted into a military aircraft. Designated as the AFI R53 (K43) the aircraft sold in healthy numbers to Chile, China, Russia and Turkey. For the latter, a new factory was established at Kayseri in Turkey which churned out quite a few Dessau-built A20s and A35s as military versions.

## Service

The first of two development prototypes, c/n 331, flew from Dessau in March 1922. By November of that year the first Soviet-built J20, designated as the Ju 20 in service, made its first flight from Leningrad and within a short space of time a further 20 were delivered to the Soviet Navy for reconnaissance duties.

A20 D-441, named *Orion*, made the first nocturnal postal flight on August 18, 1924 when it inaugurated the Berlin–Warnemünde–Stockholm route. Prior to this, mail routes had already been established between Berlin–Angora; both of these services were carried out by aircraft from the Junkers Luftverkehr and later Lufthansa.

As well as those air forces already mentioned, the type also served the Afghan, Austrian, Bulgarian, Finnish, Iranian, Spanish and Turkish Air Forces, the latter using the type the most with approximately 64 A20s taken on strength.

## Production

Approximately 186 aircraft were built in the J20 family at Dessau, Fili and Limhamn. This figure breaks down into 43 A20/A25s (Dessau), 20 A20/A25s (Fili) and 123 A35s (Limhamn).

| Technical Data – Junkers A20L, W, A, BE & B | |
| --- | --- |
| ENGINE | (L) One 177hp Mercedes D.IIIa; (W) 185hp BMW IIIs; (a) one 260hp Junkers L2; (be) 295 BMW IV; (b) one 305hp Junkers L5 |
| WINGSPAN | (L &W) 50ft 4½in; (b) 52ft 4in |
| LENGTH | (L) 27ft 2¼in; (W) 30ft 4in; (b) 26ft 10¾in |
| WING AREA | (L & W) 302sq ft; (b) 320sq ft |
| EMPTY WEIGHT | (L) 2,139lb; (W) 2,337lb; (b) 2,448lb |
| LOADED WEIGHT | (L) 5,446lb; (W) 5,865lb; (b) 3,528lb |
| MAX SPEED | (L) 112mph; (W) 106mph; (b) 127mph |
| RANGE | (L) 621 miles; (W) 559 miles; (b) 360 miles |

**Above**: Dessau-built civilian A20feL, D-392 (c/n 353) was named *Erde* during its service with Junkers LVAG between 1923 and 1926. The aircraft joined Lufthansa in 1926 and in 1934 was registered as D-IBUX until it was written off in April 1937.

**Right**: An A20W floatplane, which was powered by an 185hp BMW IIIa engine.

# J19 (T19)

## Development

From May 1922 Allied restrictions were slightly eased allowing German aircraft manufacturers to build light aircraft, such as private touring machines. Junkers took full advantage by designing the T19 and presenting it as a two/three-seat private tourer which was really veiling its true purpose as a two-seat trainer.

## Design

The Junkers T19 was the first of many aircraft designed by Ernst Zindel who was appointed as chief designer following the death of Otto Reuter in 1922. Despite the aircraft being presented as a private tourer, the aircraft's all-metal construction would prove to be far too expensive for the man in the street, compared to aircraft built from wood with a fabric covering. As a result, only three aircraft were built, and all were initially used for experimental purposes to gain more knowledge of high-wing monoplane designs with a combination of powerplants.

The T19 had a single-piece wing made up three sections, the outer sections being removable so that the aircraft could be easily transported by road. The fuselage could accommodate two passengers and a pilot in open cockpits, although the general arrangement was for just two with access provided by a door on the port side.

The first aircraft was powered by a Siemens Sh4; the second, designated the T19a, was powered by the Sh5 and the third, the T19be, was fitted with the Sh12. The second aircraft, (c/n 529) was specifically used for trialling various engines including an 80hp Armstrong Siddeley Genet and was also credited with carrying out the first air tests of the 80hp Junkers L1 in-line engine.

## Service

The first T19, D-386 *Kolibri*, undertook its maiden flight on July 14, 1922, followed by the third aircraft in March 1923 and the second aircraft the following month. Both *Kolibri* and the second aircraft, named *Zaunkoenig*, were heavily used for flight trials, the latter in particular serving as an engine test-bed. Only the second aircraft appears to have ended up in private hands – in India where it was flown until the mid-1930s.

## Production

Three T19s were built; the prototype c/n 528 serialled D-386 and named *Kolibri*; c/n 529 registered as D-389, which first flew in April 1923 and was named *Zaunkoenig* and c/n 530 first flown in March 1923 and serialled G-IAAT for service in India and again as VT-AAV. Two further aircraft, possibly to be registered as D-296 and D-234 were not completed.

| Technical Data – Junkers T19 | |
|---|---|
| ENGINE | One 123hp Siemens Halske Sh 24 or one 80hp Armstrong Siddeley Genet |
| WINGSPAN | 36ft 11in |
| LENGTH | 22ft 5½in |
| WING AREA | 205sq ft |
| EMPTY WEIGHT | 1,202lb |
| LOADED WEIGHT | 1,720lb |
| MAX SPEED | 99mph |
| CEILING | 13,100ft |
| RANGE | 261 miles |
| ACCOMMODATION | One crew and one passenger |

The first of just three T19 two/three-seat touring aircraft prior to its maiden flight in July 1922.

# J21 (T21 and H21)

## Development

A development of the T19, the J21 (later changed to T21) was a reconnaissance aircraft designed specifically for use by the Soviet Union. Despite approximately 120 being built the aircraft was not a huge success with the Soviet Air Force, the machine serving better keeping people employed in Russia.

## Design

The Zindel-designed J21 was an un-complex all-metal high-wing aircraft which was powered by an 182hp BMW IIIa engine. Work began on the aircraft, which was heavily based on the T19, in February 1923. One novel feature of the two-seater J21 was that it had fuel tanks mounted either side of the fuselage, directly below the parasol-wing, which could be jettisoned in an emergency.

## Service

The first of two prototypes built at Dessau, c/n 354, made its maiden flight in the hands of Zimmerman in June 1923. The plan was to prepare these two prototypes prior to the main production which would take place at Fili, near Moscow. However, the development period did not go smoothly and at an early stage the wing had to be completely re-designed. This entailed reducing the wing area by a third to lower the load being placed on the structure, as well as several other modifications.

By August 1923, the two prototypes were sent to Moscow from where 120 aircraft were built until 1926. Production aircraft were designated as Ju 21s but despite many entering Soviet service the aircraft was not popular due to a lack of power, even though a 295hp BMW IVa was fitted into these aeroplanes. In an attempt to keep the Russians interested, Junkers offered the aircraft with L2 and L5 engines (aircraft to be designated as the H21) but even these powerplants fell short of the original Russian requirement. Production of the H21 was to be undertaken at Dessau but this never materialised.

Many Ju 21s did see service in Russia and a handful also with the Imperial Iranian Air Force during the mid to late 1920s; while quite a few saw brief service with Dobrolet airlines and Aeroflot.

## Production

Approximately 120 J21/Ju21s were built, all but the two prototypes, c/n 354 and 355 (later serialled CCCP-122 and 121 in 1929) were manufactured at Fili, Moscow. Fili production was from c/n 356 to 406, c/n 476 to 509 and c/n 801 and 802. A further 13 had no identifiable construction numbers but where serialled CCCP-196, 197, 265, 278, 280, 218, 292 to 296 and 198.

| Technical Data – Junkers J21 (Data For BMW IIIa) | |
| --- | --- |
| ENGINE | (Prototype) One 185hp BMW IIIa; (Production Ju21) one 295hp BMW IVa |
| WINGSPAN | 35ft 1¼in |
| LENGTH | 25ft 11in |
| WING AREA | 235sq ft |
| EMPTY WEIGHT | 1,830lb |
| LOADED WEIGHT | 2,701lb |
| MAX SPEED | 135mph |
| CEILING | 13,100ft |
| RANGE | 466 miles |
| ARMAMENT | One fixed and one movable machine gun |

Emblazoned with red Russian stars under their wings, this line of Ju 21s is shown during their brief service with the Soviet Air Force in the mid-1920s.

# J23 (T23)

## Development

Presented as a two-seat trainer or general purpose aircraft for private use, the J23 (later designated as the T23) was actually an experimental aircraft built for wing load testing.

## Design

A development of the T19, the slightly larger T23 was created to gain further experience of high-wing design aircraft but could also be easily converted into a biplane to compare data gathered. The bulk of the T23 was made of duralumin, the fuselage being made up of a tubular framework which was covered in corrugated sheet. The wing was very similar to the T19 with a constant chord centre section and tapered outer sections. As a monoplane, the aircraft was designated as the T23E (E= Eindecker) with a cantilever wing which had no outboard struts. As a biplane the aircraft was the T23D (D= Doppeldecker), the lower wing being braced to the upper by a pair of V-shaped struts. Both configurations were powered by a 99 Le Rhône rotary air-cooled engine. While the T23E was marginally quicker in the air, the high-wing configuration resulted in a longer take-off run and higher speed needed to lift off.

## Service

The prototype T23, c/n 440 undertook its maiden flight in March 1923 in Doppeldecker configuration and within a few months flight testing was completed as a Eindecker. By January 1924 the fourth and

T23, c/n 440, after the aircraft was reconfigured
as a biplane during flight testing in early 1924.

final T23 had flown and it appears that the type was never intended for massed production. Even so, at least two T23s, D-391 *Falter* and D-413 *Schmetterling* went on to serve with the Fürth Flying School in northern Bavaria. The remaining two T23s were also sold to flying schools, whose identities remain unknown.

## Production

Just four aircraft were built, all at Dessau. The prototype T23, c/n 440 first flew in March 1923; c/n 441 flew in October 1923 and was registered D-413 and named *Schmetterling*; c/n 442 followed in January 1924, registered D-485 and named *Heuschrecke* and finally, c/n 443, registered as a D-391 and named *Falter*.

| Technical Data – Junkers T23D and T23E | |
| --- | --- |
| ENGINE | One 99hp Le Rhône |
| WINGSPAN | 44ft 3¼in |
| LENGTH | 23ft 9¾in |
| WING AREA | (D) 357sq ft; (E) 228sq ft |
| EMPTY WEIGHT | (D) 1,300lb; (E) 1,136lb |
| LOADED WEIGHT | (E) 1,687lb |
| MAX SPEED | (D) 77mph; (E) 87mph |
| RANGE | 112 miles |

# J22

## Development

The J22 represented another attempt by Junkers to re-equip the Soviet Air Force with an economical and easy to build aircraft. Unfortunately, the aircraft was let down by a lack of power and only two examples were built.

## Design

In order to speed up the design process, Zindel relied heavily upon the T21's parasol-wing to save development time, but as the J22 was meant to be a fighter the wing could not be mounted on struts because of the more extreme forces that would be placed upon it in combat. Therefore, Zindel positioned the wing directly on top of the fuselage, in the same position once occupied by the pilot's seat in the T21. The remaining rear gunner's cockpit, set well back in the fuselage, was now used by the pilot. The same jettisonable fuel tanks of the T21 were also fitted to the J22 but the little fighter did have a completely new tail unit. Power, which would prove to be the Achilles heel of the J22, was provided by a 182hp BMW III which was the most powerful engine allowed by Allied restrictions at the time.

## Service

The J22 prototype, c/n 407, was first flown by Wilhelm Zimmermann from Dessau on November 30, 1923 and even before the aircraft was sent to the Soviets for evaluation, it was clear that the BMW III was woefully inadequate to power a fighter. The position of the wing was a problem as well, the pilot's forward vision was poor and any enemy aircraft in its sights would be out of view from any point below the horizontal.

Various modifications were carried out on the prototype and this was followed by a second aircraft, c/n 408 which undertook its maiden flight on June 25, 1924. Despite all the effort made by Junkers to turn the J22 into an acceptable aircraft, the machine was rejected by the Soviets on many counts including poor performance and poor visibility.

The planned production of the aircraft at Fili, where it would have been designated the Ju 22 was cancelled, as was the planned Dessau production, where the aircraft would have been built as the S22, T22 and H22.

## Production

Just two aircraft were built at Dessau, the prototype, c/n 407 which first flew in November 1923 and c/n 408, first flown in June 1924 and registered as CH-128 in October 1924.

| Technical Data – Junkers J22 | |
| --- | --- |
| ENGINE | One 182hp BMW IIIa |
| WINGSPAN | 32ft 9¾in |
| LENGTH | 21ft 8in |
| WING AREA | 161sq ft |
| EMPTY WEIGHT | 1,566lb |
| LOADED WEIGHT | 2,139lb |
| MAX SPEED | 137mph |
| RANGE | 279 miles |
| ARMAMENT | Two fixed, forward-firing machine guns |

The first of just two J22 fighters built, c/n 407 is seen here before its maiden flight in November 1923. Designed for massed production in the Soviet Union, the aircraft was let down by a lack of power and a badly positioned wing.

# G23

## Development

By the mid-1920s, the highly successful F13 airliner had reached the peak of its development and rapidly growing airlines of the day began to demand an aircraft that could carry more passengers over greater distances. In 1923 Junkers put Zindel to work on a new aircraft similar to the F13, but larger. Designated as the J23 (G23) it was to be fitted with three low-powered engines (even though it was actually designed with one powerplant) in an effort to overcome the ever-present Allied restrictions.

## Design

The initial design with three 195hp Junkers L2 engines presented a problem for the Allied Commission which thought the aircraft possessed enough power to be converted into a military machine. So the G23 was redesigned to accommodate a single 185hp BMW IIIa in the nose and a pair of 160hp Mercedes D.IIIa engines, one on each wing. Although the total power output was now 15% lower than the original design the aircraft would still be able to fly if an engine failed, but its capability of being a practical load-carrying airliner was questionable.

The G23 had a tubular framework fuselage which was built integrally with the centre section of the wing. The fuselage framework was covered with X-braced longerons, and pierced metal frame formers all covered in a corrugated Duralumin skin. Control surfaces were horn balanced, and both the rudder and tailplane were fitted with trim tabs which were essential in the event of an engine failure. The wings were built in two sections, the inner carrying its own engine while the outer was attached with the tried and tested ball and socket joints.

The open cockpit had dual controls and the cabin, which could be accessed from the cockpit, had room for nine passengers. An access door was fitted on each side of the rear cabin which had six good sized windows along each flank.

## Service

Because of a lack of space at Dessau and the factory still being fully committed to F13 production, the prototype G23 (c/n 831) had its final assembly work carried out at Fuerth, Nüremburg. On September 18, 1924, Wilhelm Zimmermann carried out the maiden flight which was marred when the aircraft was damaged on landing.

As predicted the G23 was under-powered, but having built the aircraft to the letter within Allied restrictions Junkers decided that new engines could be fitted if the work was carried out at the Limhamn plant. So the few G23s that were built were flown to Limhamn and at A.B. Flygindustri the aircraft were re-engined with a trio of 305hp Junkers L5 engines, with the type being redesignated as the G24.

## Production

In total, 15 G23s were built at Dessau; these were c/n 831 to 845 and c/n 849 and 850; only the prototype c/n 831 (later registered as CH-132 (Ad Astra)) and D-1335 (Lufthansa), c/n 838 registered as S-AAAG and SE-AAG remained as G23s.

| Technical Data – Junkers G23 | |
| --- | --- |
| ENGINE | One 185hp BMW IIIa and two 160hp Mercedes D.IIIa |
| WINGSPAN | 93ft 6in |
| LENGTH | 50ft 0½in |
| WING AREA | 958sq ft |
| EMPTY WEIGHT | 7,938lb |
| LOADED WEIGHT | 13,230lb |
| MAX SPEED | 109mph |
| RANGE | 621 miles |
| ACCOMMODATION | Two crew and nine passengers |

A very rare view of G23c (c/n 845) fitted with a single 450hp Napier Lion engine mounted in the nose. This configuration was short lived as the aircraft was converted to tri-motor G24 standard at Limhamn in 1925. The aircraft briefly served with Ad Astra until 1927 before being transferred to Lufthansa, where it remained until it was wrecked in an accident in 1935.

D-UMUR at Templehof, Berlin. Originally built as a G23 (c/n 839), a busy career ensued with Ad Astra, Bayerische LV AG and finally Lufthansa. After conversion to a G24 the aircraft was finally altered to a single-engined configuration with a Junkers Jumo 4 (as per the F24kay). (*Aeroplane*)

# J26 (T26) and J27 (T27)

## Development

The J26 and J27, later redesignated as the T26 and T27 respectively, represented the end of the developmental line for the parasol wing type of aircraft. Designed as a two-seat training or sports aircraft, the T26 drew heavily on the T19 and T23 but was much more aerodynamic. Unfortunately, this did not make the aircraft any more appealing to the civilian market.

## Design

Of all-Duralumin construction the T26 was covered in a traditional corrugated surface complete with a fully braced parasol wing. Like the T23, the T26 could be fitted with a second lower wing which increased the total wing area by 55%. In the latter guise, the aircraft was designated the T26D and with just a parasol wing, the T26E.

Power for the T26 was provided by a single 83hp Junkers L1a, although a four-cylinder, air-cooled, inverted in line Argus Motoren As8 was trialled in a single T26E at one stage. The L1a engine was housed in a circular cowling, very similar in design to the T19.

A single T26E was modified to accommodate a Clerget 9Z engine in 1925 specifically for the use of an ex- World War One German fighter pilot. The aircraft was later reconfigured as a T26 and presumably had an L1a refitted.

## Service

The prototype T26 was first flown on October 23, 1923, but the aircraft's expensive all-metal construction was out of reach for the flying schools of the day and no orders were forthcoming. This did not stop eleven from being built although the majority, if not all, were confined to experimental flying duties.

At least three are credited with serving the Anhaltischer Verein F. Lufthart from June 1929 through to November 1936. These were c/n 448, registered as D-1958 and named *Muecke*, c/n 449, D-1763 named *Boelcke* and c/n 451, D-1645 christened *Blocke*. All three of these aircraft's flying careers came to end because of a crash rather than retirement!

## Production

Information about the production of the T26 and sole T27 is a little sketchy, although the general consensus is that no more than 11 were built. Other than the aircraft already mentioned above, the prototype may have been registered as D-281, one aircraft registered D-656 and named *Muecke* and two others were registered as D-665 and D-2223. Their fates are unknown.

| Technical Data – Junkers T26E and T27 | |
|---|---|
| **ENGINE** | (T26D & E) One 83hp Junkers L1a; (T26E) One 110hp Argus As8; (T27) one 128hp Clerget 9Z |
| **WINGSPAN** | (26) 44ft 3½in; (27) 43ft 1¾in |
| **LENGTH** | 24ft 8¾in |
| **WING AREA** | (26) 231sq ft; (27) 357sq ft |
| **EMPTY WEIGHT** | (26) 1,103lb; |
| **LOADED WEIGHT** | (26) 1,160lb |
| **MAX SPEED** | 81mph |
| **RANGE** | 214 miles |

By far the best looking, and most likely better performing of all the Junkers parasol-wing designs, the aircraft became the victim of its own expensive construction when it tried to break into the civilian flying scene in Germany in 1923.

# J30 (K30/R42)

## Development

The first military versions of the successful G24 family of aircraft arrived in late 1924 in the shape of the G3S1 24 air ambulance, which was a conversion of the civilian G24ba. Reconnaissance and bomber variants also began to materialise, despite Allied restrictions still being in place preventing the construction of military aircraft.

## Design

Following the appearance of the air ambulance variant in November 1924 Junkers' next offering, designed by Zindel and Pohlmann, was a single-engined reconnaissance aircraft designated as the G1Sa 24. The bomber version followed in 1925 based on the civilian G24he and redesignated as the G2sB 24. It was this latter aircraft that became the basis for the main bomber variant, known as the K30 which would be developed at Dessau, but in order to navigate around the Allied restrictions would be built in Sweden at Linhamn by A.B. Flygindustri.

The Soviets ordered 23 K30s, the bombers' parts all being sent from Dassau to Linhamn where, once constructed, they were designated as the R42. The aircraft were fitted with a pair of 7.62mm machine guns positioned in the upper fuselage, one in a forward position in the fuselage and another further back. A ventral 'dustbin', which could be lowered in the air, contained at least one more 7.62mm machine gun. 1,100lb of bombs were carried on racks below the fuselage and wings rather than in a bomb bay.

A single-engined bomber version, designated the K30do (similar to the G1Sa 24), was planned to be powered by a Jumo 4, but none were built.

## Service

In 1926 Junkers were building civilian G24s at Dessau and flying them direct to Limhamn for conversion to R42 standard. G24 conversions were also carried out at Fili and by 1927 the Soviets had received their full complement of 23 R42s which in service were redesignated as the TB2 and/or the JuG-1.

Orders were also received from the Chilean, Spanish and Yugoslav Air Forces for the R42, all of these being built at Dessau as by then Allied restrictions had either been lifted, or were being flouted to such a degree implementation proved to be impossible.

The G24 family were no strangers to setting records and the K30 contributed when one aircraft, fitted with floats, set three new records in endurance, range and speed on August 6, 1927. Carrying a payload of 2,205lb the K30 achieved a maximum speed of 106mph, covered a distance of 730 miles and remained in the air 10hrs 42min 45sec.

## Production

In total, 35 R42s were built; 23 of these were ordered by the Soviets as TB2/JuG-1s; six R42s were delivered to the Chilean Air Force, three to the Spanish Air Force and two to the Yugoslavian Air Force. An unknown number of civilian G34s were converted to R42 standard but it is presumed that these were part of the Soviet order.

| Technical Data – Junkers K30 | |
|---|---|
| ENGINE | Three 305hp Junkers L5 |
| WINGSPAN | 84ft 11¾in |
| LENGTH | 50ft 2½in |
| WING AREA | 1,018sq ft |
| EMPTY WEIGHT | 8,344lb; |
| LOADED WEIGHT | 13,737lb |
| MAX SPEED | 109mph |
| RANGE | 621 miles |
| ARMAMENT | Five 7.62mm machine guns and up to 1,102lb in bombs |

A good example of a Soviet Air Force TB2/JuG-1 fitted with a pair of floats. The R42 family could also be equipped with skis or a conventional land-based undercarriage. The Soviet Air Force operated 23 examples from 1927 up to the late 1930s.

# J24 (G24) and F24 (W41)

## Development
Going on to become the backbone of air transport in Germany, the more powerful G23 flouted the Allied restrictions and set Junkers on the path to success in the commercial airliner market.

## Design
Slightly larger than the G23, the latest Junkers airliner incorporated the same construction techniques of its predecessor and included a new ten-spar cantilever wing. Initially, power for the first G23 conversion was by a trio of 230hp Junkers L2a engines although later variants raised the bar with three 310hp L5s or a combination of a pair of L2as and a single L5 in the nose. Bespoke engine configurations also included three 380hp Jupiters in the G24a and a few aircraft, operating in Italy, were fitted with a single 500hp Isolta-Fraschini Asso.

Accommodation, like the G23, was for nine passengers in a comfortable enclosed cabin which was now the same for the crew – their days of being exposed in a semi-open cockpit were over, as the flight deck was now fully enclosed.

Several G24s were later converted to F24ko standard which involved the fitment of a single BMW VIU engine and a shorter span wing. This work was undertaken between 1928 and 1930, although by 1933 the majority were converted again with a single Jumo 4 engine, to be re-designated as the F24kay. The bulk of these aircraft remained in Lufthansa service until the beginning of World War Two.

## Service
The G24 was incorporated into airline service seamlessly in the early part of its career – still referred to as the G23 until 1926, to keep the Allied inspectors at bay. Many aircraft set aviation records during their early service including a pair of aircraft, D-901 and D-903, which undertook a 12,427-mile round trip from Berlin to Peking to investigate a new route to the Far East via Siberia. The journey was carried out between July 24 and October 26 without a single technical problem with each aircraft racking up 140 flying hours. Between April and June 1927 alone eleven aviation records tumbled when a G24 powered by L2 engines established new endurance and distance records with 1,205lb, 2,205lb and 4,409lb payloads.

Lufthansa was, unsurprisingly, the highest user of the G24 commencing in 1926 with 18 on strength for European services and, after acquiring more aircraft, routes were also established in South America. Several more were bought from the German Air Ministry in 1927 and the G24 was not phased out of Lufthansa service until 1934.

The type was also heavily used in Sweden in landplane and seaplane configurations, not to mention operators in Afghanistan, Chile, Finland, Greece, Spain and Turkey to name a few.

## Production
There were 56 aircraft G24s built/converted; approximately half were built at Dessau and half by A.B. Flygindustri at Limhamn. Eleven G24s were modified to F24 standard between 1928 and 1930.

| Technical Data – Junkers G24, CE, HE, HE-W (Floats) and F24KO | |
|---|---|
| **ENGINE** | Three 305hp Junkers L5; three 630hp BMW VIu; (ko) one 630hp BMW VIu |
| **WINGSPAN** | (ce) 97ft 9in; (he & he-W) 96ft 4in; (ko) 84ft 11¾in |
| **LENGTH** | (ce) 50ft 4in; (he) 51ft 10in; (he-W) 54ft 9½in; (ko) 50ft 0½in |
| **WING AREA** | (ce) 1,018sq ft; (he & he-W) 1,065sq ft; (ko) 852sq ft |

**Above:** An early example of a G24 which was originally built as a G23. The semi-enclosed cockpit was fully enclosed in the production version.

**Right:** This G24ba was originally named *Helvetia* in Bayerische LV AG service before being sold to Ad Astra and finally Lufthansa, with whom it is appropriately serving the Zurich route.

# J29 (T29)

## Development

The J29 did not look much of an aircraft on the surface, but it was actually one of the most pioneering machines that Junkers had built since first venturing into the aviation industry.

## Design

Designed by Zindel, the J29 introduced a 'Doppelflügel' (Double-wing) control surface which would go on to be outstandingly effective on the G38 airliner, the Ju 52 and the Ju87. The control surface consisted of a full-span aileron which was attached to the trailing edge and slightly lower than the wing, effectively forming a slot. On landing the aileron could be lowered like a flap which gave excellent control at low speeds.

The system, which was patented in 1921 (DRP No.396621), had been designed in several different ways including a double-aileron configuration giving the wing a pair of slots and more flap area when lowered. Another version of the single slotted aileron was linked to the elevator so that when the ailerons/flaps were dropped the aircraft automatically entered a nose up attitude before landing.

The two-seat J29 also featured a side-by-side seating arrangement and the crew was protected by a substantial fairing which was said to resemble the handle of a flat iron. This feature gave the aircraft its nickname of 'Bügeleisen' (Hot Iron). Built entirely of corrugated Duralumin, the J29, redesignated the T29 once built, was powered by a single 83hp Junkers L1a engine.

## Service

The first of just two T29s built made its maiden flight on April 22, 1925, followed by the second not long after. It is believed that the aircraft was redesignated from the 'J' to the 'T', to give the impression that aircraft could be used in a training role. It is not clear how much serious promotion work Junkers carried out, but it was clear that the two aircraft, in the flight test role, were more valuable to the company than a handful of potential civilian or even military sales.

## Production

Two aircraft, presumably the prototype was c/n 911 as the second aircraft was definitely c/n 912, were built and flight tested from Dessau. The first aircraft was later registered as D-657 and the second D-666; the latter is believed to have continued in the flight test role until 1932.

| Technical Data – J29 | |
| --- | --- |
| ENGINE | One 83hp Junkers L1a |
| WINGSPAN | 37ft 8¾in |
| LENGTH | 23ft 5½in |
| WING AREA | 191sq ft |
| EMPTY WEIGHT | 1,080lb |
| LOADED WEIGHT | 1,654lb |
| MAX SPEED | 87mph |
| RANGE | 292 miles |

# J32 (A32) and K39

## Development

A spin-off from the A20/25/35 family of aircraft, the J32 (A32) was a slightly smaller machine designed by Zindel and Karl Plauth. The three-seat A32 was built to be either a mail plane or a photographic reconnaissance aircraft, the extra seat being occupied by an air gunner in response to experienced gained in combat with the J21.

## Design

The A32 civilian prototype was a low-wing monoplane, covered in corrugated Duralumin with the exception of the forward fuselage which had a smooth metal covering. Power was provided by a 490hp BMW VI engine which was later replaced by a 640hp Junkers L55; the aircraft being referred to as the A32ba with this powerplant. Engine cooling was provided by a prominent radiator positioned directly under the nose behind the wooden propeller. The wings incorporated the double-wing system with full-span ailerons while the rudder and elevator were both horn balanced.

A more aggressive version of the A32 was also designed by Junkers and designated as the K39. It is believed that the second of only two A32s built was used as the prototype K39, the work being carried at by A.B. Flygindustri at Limhamn because of the military nature of the aircraft. The K39 featured a pair of fixed forward-firing machine guns and a fourth crew position for a bomb aimer in a gondola attached to the lower fuselage, thus making the aircraft not only an armed reconnaissance aircraft, but also a bomber. The K39 was powered by the standard A32's BMW VI and an L55 and L88 engine was also trialled.

## Service

The first prototype, which was also the first aircraft to be fitted with a 'Vee' configuration power plant, made its maiden flight from Dessau in 1926. The aircraft provided Junkers with a lot of useful data, but no orders were forthcoming for the A32 or the K39. Sadly, the second A32, after its conversion to a K39, was lost on November 2, 1927 whilst Karl Plauth was testing the aircraft with an L55 engine. Despite Plauth being a proficient sport pilot he was unable to fully recover the aircraft from a loop; the company's promising young designer was killed and the aircraft destroyed.

## Production

Two aircraft were built at Dessau, the prototype c/n 3100 and c/n 3101, the latter being registered as D-1155 in 1926. This aircraft was despatched to Limhamn and converted to the K29 prototype by A.B. Flygindustri and serialled S-27.

| Technical Data – A32 and K39 | |
| --- | --- |
| ENGINE | (A32) One 490hp BMW VI; (K39) one Junkers L 55 |
| WINGSPAN | 58ft 4¾in |
| LENGTH | 36ft 5in |
| WING AREA | (A32) 441sq ft; (K39) 431sq ft |
| EMPTY WEIGHT | (A32) 4,101lb; (K39) 4,741lb |
| LOADED WEIGHT | (A32) 6,009lb; (K39) 7,673lb |
| MAX SPEED | (A32) 137mph; (K39) 143mph |
| CEILING | 19,700ft |
| RANGE | (A32) 348 miles; (K39) 515 miles |

The first of only two A32s built was not given a civilian serial and was identifiable only by its construction number – c/n 3101. The A32 featured many firsts, including its smooth steel covering – it was the first Junkers aircraft since World War One to dispense with the traditional corrugated method.

# J33 (W33)

## Development

Another successful development of the F13 was the W33 which was specifically designed for air cargo operations. A very advanced machine, both regarding its construction and aerodynamics, the W33 was produced in more than 30 variations.

## Design

The W33 differed from the F13 in several ways, the most significant being a new flat-topped and lowered fuselage – without windows, as the aircraft was initially designed solely for cargo work. However, later variants were used for cargo and passenger operations and as a result sliding-type windows were installed.

As already mentioned, a huge range of variants were produced beginning with the prototype W33 which was powered by a 305hp Junkers L5 engine. The W33a was followed by the W33b with a bigger cargo hold powered by the L5 and the W33ba powered by the L2. The W33be and W33ce was a W33 fitted with a BMW Va engine and the L5-powered W33c had a modified and strengthened central wing section.

The wing of the W33d was larger and slightly swept back while the W33f introduced another version of the wing a fully enclosed cockpit and a window in the cargo hold. The W33fa employed the Jupiter IX engine, and the W33fei and W33gao, the Siemens SH 20 power plant. Various other changes included an extended fuselage, a fully enclosed cockpit and stronger undercarriage.

## Service

The prototype W33 (a floatplane), c/n 794 registered D-921 and named *Schildrähe*, was first flown by Zimmermann on June 17, 1926 from the River Elbe at Leopoldshafen. The first production aircraft, registered D-1048, appeared in early 1927 – a year that witnessed the W33 complete several record-breaking flights.

On March 16, 1927, the German pilot Schnäbele in a W33L, flew for 15hrs 57mins with a 1,102lb payload followed by Junkers Chief Test Pilot Loose, who flew for 14hrs 8mins, three days later over a distance of 1,057 miles in a W33 seaplane. On March 21, Loose and Schnäbele flew a W33L landplane over a distance of 1,700 miles in 22hrs 11mins to set another record. The world endurance record fell again on July 5 when Zimmermann and Risztics flew a W33L for 65hrs 25mins which was followed by Riztics and Edzard on August 3 who flew for 52hrs 22mins over a distance of 2,895 miles.

The most famous record achieved by a W33 came on April 12, 1928, when Koehl, Von Hunefeld and Fitzmaurice in D-1167 *Bremen* made the first East to West crossing of the Atlantic. The trio took off from Baldonnel near Dublin and after 36hrs in the air, landed safely at Greenly Island, Labrador.

## Production

There were 199 built; the majority at Dessau although several were also manufactured at Limhamn and Fili. Those W33s registered in Russia were redesignated as the PS-3; those built at Fili were designated PS-4s and in Swedish Air Force service the type was renamed as Trp2.

| Technical Data – W33B | |
| --- | --- |
| ENGINE | One 305hp Junkers L5 |
| WINGSPAN | 60ft 2½in |
| LENGTH | 34ft 5½in |
| WING AREA | 463sq ft |
| EMPTY WEIGHT | 2,646lb |
| LOADED WEIGHT | 4,631lb |
| MAX SPEED | 121mph |
| CEILING | 14,100ft |
| RANGE | 621 miles |

**Above**: Junkers W33c, D-1642 demonstrates the aircraft's use as a crop sprayer at Dessau in 1927.

**Right**: Purchased by US millionaire Charles Levine, W33 NX7465 (c/n 2516) *Queen of the Air* was used for the failed attempt to cross the Atlantic from Berlin via Lisbon and the Azores to New York in August/September 1931. The aircraft, which was registered as D-2072 and named *Esa* for the attempt, had to ditch into the sea where the three crew spent several days on the floating aircraft before they were rescued.

# J31 (G31)

## Development

In 1926, designers Zindel and Hofmann set about re-working the G24 into an aircraft with a higher carrying capacity. As always, the new aircraft, designated as the J31 (G31) was one of the most advanced of the age, but it was still outshone by the commercially successful G24 and as a result only 13 were built.

## Design

A three-engined all-metal cantilever monoplane, the G31 had a capacious fuselage which could carry 15 passengers; the majority, three abreast. The prototype G31 was powered by three 310hp Junkers L5 water-cooled inline engines with a single radiator mounted under the nose while production aircraft tendered to be powered by less complex air-cooled radials such as the Jupiter or Hornet.

The G31 also featured a full-span double-wing, twin fins and rudders mounted on a braced tailplane. The fuselage, which could not only be configured for passengers, was also designed for an air ambulance role for stretcher cases or when operated at night, beds could be fitted. All seats and their fittings, including the fuselage inner lining could be removed for pure freighter work. Access to the fuselage was usually via side doors, but in the case of one aircraft (VH-UOW) a large hatch was provided, 11ft 10in long and the full width of the fuselage, behind the cockpit for awkward sized loads.

Another novel feature of the G31 was a tunnel which ran from under the cockpit to the rear fuselage giving access to vital control rods and wiring during flight.

## Service

The first G31 (c/n 3000), registered as D-1073, undertook its maiden flight on September 13, 1926, and on February 28, 1928 Lufthansa took delivery of its first G31, D-1310 named *Hermann Köhl*. By the following year eight G31s were in service with Lufthansa on long-range routes, and at least one aircraft was employed on regular nocturnal flight to airports in Scandinavia.

In production form the majority of aircraft were built to G31fo standard, powered by a trio of BMW Hornet engines. The G31 was an outstanding design but sadly a commercial failure, mainly because the G24 was much cheaper for the performance it delivered. Apart from Lufthansa a few more G31s were sold; one aircraft to Ölag Airways in Austria, a single aircraft to Guinea Airways and a pair to the Bulolo Gold Dredging Company based in Australia.

The G31 did take the prize of being the 1,000th Junkers aircraft built when, on May 24, 1928, a G31de (c/n 3003) for Ölag named *Oesterreich*, was completed.

## Production

Thirteen G31s were built between 1926 and 1930 at Dessau in the c/n range No. 3000 to 30012.

| Technical Data – G31 and G31FO | |
| --- | --- |
| **ENGINE** | Three 305hp Junkers L5; (fo) three 525hp BMW Hornet |
| **WINGSPAN** | 99ft 5in |
| **LENGTH** | 56ft 8¼in |
| **WING AREA** | 1,098sq ft |
| **EMPTY WEIGHT** | 11,576lb |
| **LOADED WEIGHT** | 18,743lb |
| **MAX SPEED** | 130mph |
| **CEILING** | (fo) 14,100ft |
| **RANGE** | 621 miles |
| **ACCOMMODATION** | Up to five crew and 15 passengers |

Junkers G31fo (c/n 3008), D-1722 named *Brandenburg*, not long after it was delivered to Lufthansa in 1929. Sold to RLM in early 1936 the aircraft came to a tragic end when it was destroyed after a mid-air collision with Ju 52, D-APUT.

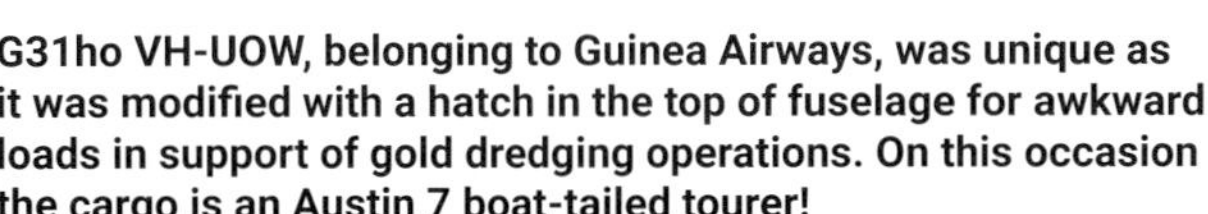

G31ho VH-UOW, belonging to Guinea Airways, was unique as it was modified with a hatch in the top of fuselage for awkward loads in support of gold dredging operations. On this occasion the cargo is an Austin 7 boat-tailed tourer!

# J34 (W34) (Inc. Ju 46)

## Development

First flown only a few weeks after the prototype W33, the slightly larger W34 was a more versatile variant which offered customers a wide range of power plants. It was built in very large numbers for both civilian and military customers and many examples were still serving into the early 1960s.

## Design

The development of the W34 ran concurrently with that of the W33, the former differing in many ways. Cabin windows were fitted into the W34, but the only major difference in the prototype was more power from a 470hp Gnome et Rhône Jupiter air-cooled radial. The production aircraft were where changes were introduced, the aircraft having a slightly higher fuselage roof and the whole tail unit a greater surface area.

Production aircraft were powered by a host of different engines including the Bristol Jupiter VI, VII and XI, BMW Hornet, Siemens Sh20, Pratt & Whitney Wasp and the Armstrong Siddeley Jaguar.

In 1932, the W34 was re-designed slightly by Zindel and Pohlmann and redesignated as the Ju 46. Specially prepared for cross-Atlantic postal flights by Lufthansa, the aircraft was re-stressed and reinforced to cope with a catapult launch from the NDL liners 'Europa' and 'Bremen'. Only five were built, the first of them Ju46fi, D-2271 'Bremen' was delivered in March 1932.

## Service

The prototype W34, D-922 was first flown by Zimmermann on July 7, 1926, and it was not long before the type was ordered by airlines and air forces across the world. The W34, like the W33, also achieved several aviation records, beginning with a new world speed record on May 11, 1927, with Georg Jueterbock at the controls. Altitude records also fell on September 14, 1928, when a W34, once again flown by Jueterbock, reached an altitude of 30,150ft with a 1,100lb payload. On May 26, 1929, Willy Neuenhofen, in a W34be, reached 41,794ft in 45 minutes, beating the altitude record again.

The W34 saw widespread military service including action as an improvised bomber with the Colombian Air Force during their skirmish with Peru in 1932 and three, designated as the Trp2A, served with the Swedish Air Force from 1933 to 1953. The type saw extensive service in the Luftwaffe in very large numbers as an advanced flight trainer, blind flying trainer and radio trainer. It was also used as a general communications and transport aircraft. Incredibly, over 600 W34s were still on Luftwaffe strength by the beginning of 1944.

## Production

Production figures for the W34, were approximately 1,000 built for the civilian market and approximately 2,000 plus for military customers between 1926 and 1935. The five Ju 46s were built in 1932. The aircraft were all built by Junkers at Dessau until 1934 and at A.B. Flygindustri Limhamn until 1935. However, military variants were also built under licence by Arado, Dornier, Henschel, HFB, MIAG and Weser; these companies produced just under 2,000 aircraft alone.

| Technical Data – W34B | |
| --- | --- |
| ENGINE | One 420hp Jupiter VI |
| WINGSPAN | 60ft 2½in |
| LENGTH | 34ft 5½in |
| WING AREA | 495sq ft |
| EMPTY WEIGHT | 2,591lb |
| LOADED WEIGHT | 4,090lb |
| MAX SPEED | 124mph |
| CEILING | 20,700ft |
| RANGE | 528-560 miles |
| ACCOMMODATION | Two crew and six passengers |

**Above**: Several W34s served in Canada, and many were still flying into the early 1960s, including CF-ARI, here in service with Canadian Airways.

**Right**: A dramatic image of Ju 46, D-UBUS *Europa* being catapult-launched from the liner *Bremen* over 900 miles off the US coast. The all-red seaplanes could shave a whole day of the delivery of post in either direction across the Atlantic.

Registered as 'D-4' purely for its delivery flight to Eurasia Airlines in China, this aircraft is a W34gi (c/n 2737) was to be re-registered as EU-III. However, the BMW Hornet-powered aircraft never made it to China, crashing in Germany on April 29, 1933.

LUFT HANSA

# J36 (S36) and K37 (KI-1 and 2)

## Development

The only twin-engined aircraft to be designed by Hugo Junkers and Ernst Zindel, the S36 was a development of the A32 and was intended to be used as a mailplane. However, as with the majority of Junkers aircraft produced from the late 1920s onwards, an alternative and perhaps more pertinent military role was never far away.

## Design

The S36 started out as a low-wing twin-engined aircraft with twin fins and rudders, three open cockpits and a fixed undercarriage. Duralumin skinned over a metal structure, the fuselage incorporated the centre section of the wing for added strength, while the outer wing sections were attached by spherical couplings. A pair of un-cowled 440hp Jupiter VI air-cooled radials provided the power for the S36.

Only two S36s were built and the first of these was flown to Limhamn where A.B. Flygindustri militarised the aircraft to become the prototype K37. The aircraft was converted with a reconnaissance role in mind; work included the fitment of a single machine gun in the open rear cockpit and another in the open front cockpit which was glazed around the front. A third machine gun was also mounted below the rear fuselage, this being operated remotely via levers and pulleys by the rear gunner, or it could be manually fired in a kneeling position. Armament was later increased to seven machine-guns in various fixed positions. Bomb racks were fitted below each wing, capable of carrying four 27½lb and eight 110lb bombs; these were aimed onto the target by the front gunner. An aerial camera was fitted into the lower fuselage and this was also operated by the front gunner.

One K37 was transferred to Japan in 1931 resulting in a production licence being bought by Mitsubishi. The aircraft was manufactured in two versions, the Ki-1 heavy bomber and the Ki-2 light bomber. Barely resembling the original K37, the Ki-1 was a much larger aircraft powered by a pair of 926hp Mitsubishi Ha-2 engines. The Ki-2 was more in keeping with the original design and was powered by a pair of Mitsubishi Ha-8 diesel engines which were neatly cowled. A modified version, designated as the Ki-2-2, featured a retractable undercarriage.

## Service

The prototype S36 (c/n 3200) completed its maiden flight on September 5, 1927, followed by a second, which was registered as S-AABP and sent to Limhamn where it was converted into the prototype K37. A second K37 is believed to have been built and one if not both K37s were sent to Japan in February 1931. The Ki-1 made its maiden flight in August 1932 followed by the first Ki-2 in May 1933. Details of Japanese service are sketchy but it is clear that the Ki-1 was replaced in 1936 by the Fiat Br.20, while the Ki-2 was still regarded by the Allies as being in service during World War Two, albeit in a training role, because it received the code name 'Louise'.

## Production

Two S36s were manufactured; one being later converted to K37 standard while possibly one K37 was built from scratch. Under licence Mitsubishi and Kawasaki built 219 Ki-1s, 126 Ki-2s and 61 Ki-2-2s in Japan between 1933 and 1936.

| Technical Data – S36 and KI-1 | |
| --- | --- |
| ENGINE | (36) Two 440hp Jupiter VI; (1) two 940hp Mitsubishi Ha-2 |
| WINGSPAN | (36) 66ft 1¼in; (1) 86ft 11½in |
| LENGTH | (36) 37ft 4¾in; (1) 48ft 6½in |
| WING AREA | (36) 581sq ft; (1) 976.72sq ft |
| EMPTY WEIGHT | (36) 5,733lb; (1) 10,759lb |
| LOADED WEIGHT | (36) 9,482lb; (1) 17,857lb |
| MAX SPEED | (36) 158mph; (1) 137mph |
| SERVICE CEILING | (36) 29,500ft; (1) 16,404ft |
| RANGE | (36) 590 miles; (1) 683 miles |

*Above*: The fully militarised S26 prototype, originally registered as D-1252, re-registered as S-AABL in Sweden and then as D-AMIX in 1934 for service with the Luftwaffe as a bomber trainer.

*Right*: Built by Mitsubishi and Kawasaki under licence in Japan, 187 Ki-2 and Ki-2-2s were manufactured between 1933 and 1936. In Japanese service the Ki-2 was designated as the 'Army Type 93-1 Twin-engine Light Bomber'.

# K43

## Development

The K43 was a militarised general-purpose aircraft which was primarily intended to be operated in the reconnaissance and/or light bomber role. Converted from a standard Junkers W34, only a few K43s were built, but all were gainfully employed in Northern Europe and across South America

## Design

The military conversion of the W34 to K43 standard was carried out by A.B. Flygindustri at Limhamn between 1927 and 1933. The spacious fuselage of the all-metal W34 was easy to convert for military operations and could be offered to customers in a wide range of versions. The aircraft could be configured as a standard landplane, a seaplane or in the case of the Finnish Air Force, it could also operate on skis.

Modifications included three open cockpits, the rear two being occupied by gunners and the forward by two pilots. The latter position could be open or fully enclosed depending upon the variant being converted. Military ordnance included bombs and depth charges up to a maximum weight of 440lbs, these presumably being carried on under wing or possibly under-fuselage racks.

Power for the landplane variant was provided by a 450hp Jupiter VI and the seaplane, which needed more grunt to get off the water, was fitted with a 500hp Siemens Jupiter. The seaplane variant was also fitted with a slightly revised wing and had a bigger fin and rudder.

## Service

It is not clear exactly when the first K43 took to the air, other than it was sometime in 1927. The first military customer is unknown, but the Finnish Air Force, which ordered six K43Fs (serialled Ju-122 to Ju-127), took delivery from 1931 and incredibly the type was not retired until 1952. The Finns made the most of their aircraft and the six machines were operated in the land, sea and ski configuration throughout their lengthy careers.

The type also served in small numbers with the Argentinian and Chilean Air Forces, at least two K43Ws also served with the Portuguese Navy and also the Bolivian Air Force. It was whilst serving with the latter that the type gained the nickname of the 'Bush Bomber' following its extensive use during the Chaco War between Bolivia and Paraguay which lasted from 1932 to 1935. At least one K43 was in Luftwaffe service from 1931.

## Production

Eighteen K43s were built/converted at Limhamn between 1927 and 1933.

| Technical Data – K43 Landplane and Seaplane | |
|---|---|
| **ENGINE** | (L) One 450hp Jupiter VI; (S) One 500hp Siemens Jupiter |
| **WINGSPAN** | (L) 58ft 6in; (S) 58ft 3½in |
| **LENGTH** | 33ft 7in |
| **WING AREA** | (L) 474sq ft; (S) 468sq ft |
| **EMPTY WEIGHT** | (L) 3,538lb; (S) 3,308lb |
| **MAX LOADED WEIGHT** | (L) 7,056lb; (S) 4,630lb |
| **MAX SPEED** | (L) 140mph; (S) 126mph |
| **CEILING** | (L) 17,400ft; (S) 23,000ft |
| **RANGE** | 683 miles |
| **ARMAMENT** | (L) Two machine guns and up to 441lb of bombs; (S) two to three machine guns, depth charges and splinter bombs |

Possibly the sole K43 to see Luftwaffe service was this example with an enclosed cockpit, a single dorsal machine gun position and complex camouflage.

The first K43 to be delivered to Finland was JU-122, seen here as a seaplane. The Finns made good use of their small fleet of K43s, the last was not retired until 1952.

# J47 (K47) and J48 (A48)

## Development
As the first Junkers aircraft since the end of World War One to be designed as military machines from the outset, the A48 and K47 would give Germany a taste of future military tactics.

## Design
Originally designed by Karl Plauth in early 1927, the late pilot's work was continued by his assistant Hermann Pohlmann. The A48 had an all-metal airframe, but rather than the traditional all-over corrugated surface, the fuselage was finished in smooth alloy, while only the wings and remaining surfaces were of ribbed Duralumin. The aircraft was a monoplane, but this was bolstered by substantial under wing bracing struts which attached to an equally solid undercarriage. The aircraft had a single fin and rudder and power was supplied by various engines. These included a BMW Hornet in the A48ba, the A48b and be was powered by a Jupiter VII, the A48bi by the Jupiter VI, the A48c had a Armstrong Siddeley Jaguar, the A48da a BMW Hornet, the A48dy a Siemens Sh20 and the A48fy a Siemens Jupiter VI.

The K47 mainly differed from the K48 by having a twin-tail arrangement to give an air gunner a better field of fire from the rear cockpit. Bombs could be fitted on underwing racks and like the A48 before it; the K47 was fitted with a host of air-cooled radial engines which as well those already listed included the American-produced Pratt & Whitney Wasp.

## Service
The A48 prototype, registered D-1057, made its maiden flight in 1928 and like its successors was heavily employed in test flying and trials with different power plants. Trials with slightly swept back wings were carried out by D-2012 during 1930 and 1931. In 1932, D-2284, fitted with metal dive breaks, performed the world's first dive-bombing tests at Breslau. These trials effectively paved the way for the iconic Ju87 'Stuka' which made the terrifying tactic of dive-bombing into an art form. Several A48s were also tested by the Soviets at Lipzek but only two were actually purchased, the only other sale being a single aircraft, c/n 3354, to a customer in South America.

The conversion of several A48s to K47 standard was carried out at Limhamn. The prototype, registered S-AABW, first flew in late 1928 but expected high sales never materialised. Only twelve aircraft were sold to China, a few to Russia and a single aircraft may have ended up in Japan. A few K47s were employed by the Luftwaffe as experimental and training aircraft up to the beginning of World War Two.

## Production
Approximately 30 examples of the A48 and K47 were built at Dessau (A48) and Limhamn (K47) between 1927 and 1933.

| Technical Data – A48 and K47 | |
|---|---|
| ENGINE | (48) One 500hp Siemens Jupiter; (47) one 480hp Bristol Jupiter |
| WINGSPAN | (48) 40ft 8in; (47) 40ft 8¼in |
| LENGTH | 28ft 0½in |
| HEIGHT | (48) 9ft 2½in; (47) 8ft 6¼in |
| WING AREA | 245sq ft |
| EMPTY WEIGHT | (48) 2,403lb; (47) 2,282lb |
| LOADED WEIGHT | (48) 3,638lb; (47) 3,605lb |
| MAX SPEED | (48) 165mph; (47) 180mph |
| CEILING | (48) 24,600ft; (47) 26,000ft |
| RANGE | (48) 310 miles; (47) 298 miles |
| ARMAMENT | (47) Three machine guns |

Junkers A48 D-2012 (c/n 3365) after its single tail was replaced by the twin fin arrangement which would be the hallmark of the K47. This was the aircraft that carried out the world's first dive-bombing experiments at Breslau in 1932.

# J50 (A50) 'Junior'

## Development

Originally developed under the designation EF31, the idea of a two-seat all-metal sports tourer designed to compete with traditional wood and canvas types, was first presented by Heinrich Johann Arntzen in late 1928. Hugo Junkers was not, at first, very enthusiast about the idea, following previous attempts to build such types of aircraft. However, Junkers asked that Pohlmann check over the designs to see if the idea was plausible.

## Design

Re-designated as the J50, later changed to the A50 'Junior', the aircraft was a pretty looking low-wing cantilever monoplane of all-corrugated Duralumin construction. The 'Junior' had a semi-monocoque fuselage with provision for two people in separate tandem cockpits and room for 66lb of luggage as per the original specification.

Another part of the original specification stated that the aircraft should have an endurance of up to five hours and to help achieve this, fuel was carried in a pair of 8-gallon tanks in the wing centre section and a third 2½ gallon gravity tank located between the forward cockpit and the engine. Power, for the prototype at least, was provided by a 60hp Junkers David light oil engine or a 50hp Anzani radial, while production machines where generally fitted with the 87hp Armstrong Siddeley Genet or the 79hp Walter Vega.

## Service

The maiden flight of the A50 took place on February 13, 1929, and was believed to have been flown by Arntzen. Following an intense marketing programme, hopes were high that big orders would come in (as optimistic as 6,000) and as a result, Junkers confidently built five development prototypes.

During 1930 the A50 was heavily demonstrated beginning in May when one aircraft was flown across Austria for a total distance of 3,105 miles, visiting a host of airfields where, 100 take-off and landings were carried out without incident. Records were broken by the A50 D-1896 as well, beginning on June 4 when Zimmermann and Reginald Schinzinger broke the class altitude record by flying to 15,134ft. The same day Zimmermann, flying alone, raised the bar to 18,571ft. With its fuel capacity raised to 31 gallons, D-1896 also broke the endurance record on June 6 when Grundke and passenger remain aloft for 8hr 27min. Grundke flying solo raised this record to 16hr 9min just a week later.

Japanese pilot Seijiro Yoshihara set another incredible record between August 20 and 29, 1930, when he flew A50ce D-3 (re-registered J-BECB in Japan) the 7,204 miles from Berlin to Tokyo. German aviatrix Marga von Etzdorf carried out the same journey in August 1931 but had already set records of her own by flying an A50 from Berlin to Tenerife in November 1931. Another amazing A50 record was set by the Finn, Bremer, who flew A50, OH-ABB from Helsingfors to Cape Town and back to Dessau in 232 flying hours!

## Production

Sadly, the 6,000-strong production run never materialised and only 69 were built and sold at an average price of £795 each for the land version. Those aircraft sold were spread across the globe including Australia, Brazil, Finland, Japan, Portugal, South Africa and Switzerland.

| Technical Data – A50 | |
| --- | --- |
| ENGINE | One 87hp Armstrong Siddeley Genet; one 79hp Walter Vega |
| WINGSPAN | 32ft 9½in |
| LENGTH | 23ft 4in |
| HEIGHT | 7ft 10½in |
| WING AREA | 147sq ft |
| EMPTY WEIGHT | 750lb |
| LOADED WEIGHT | 1,301lb |
| MAX SPEED | 102mph |
| CEILING | 13,776ft |
| RANGE | 373 miles |
| ENDURANCE | 5 hours |

The two-seat A50 sports-tourer was an attractive looking cantilever monoplane, but despite an intensive and expensive marketing campaign which including promoting the type via car showrooms and garages, only 69 examples of the 'Junior' were sold.

# J38 (G38) and K51 (Mitsubishi KI-20)

## Development

The concept of a large passenger-carrying flying-wing was first patented by Hugo Junkers in February 1910. Junkers' dream of such an aircraft nearly materialised after World War One when he began work on the JG1 project, only for it to be closed down by the Allied Commission. Further efforts emerged with the ambitious J1000 project in 1925, which was a design for an aircraft with a span of over 260ft and a wing that was 7ft 6½in deep and capable of carrying the majority of its 100-passenger capacity within it. The design eventually emerged as the smaller G38 which was the culmination of a two-decade long dream of Hugo Junkers.

## Design

The G38 featured a wing of 3,220sq ft with a chord of 32ft 9½in and a thickness at the root of 5ft 7in which was sufficient height to provide passenger seating and good access to the powerplants in flight. Power for the prototype was provided by a pair of coupled 800hp Junkers L88 Vee-cylinder engines in the inboard positions and two 400hp Junkers L8 in the outboard positions driving two and four-bladed propellers respectively. The engines were set deep into the leading edge of the wing and their oil coolers and radiators could be extended out into the air flow from under the wing.

Construction was in keeping with previous Junkers aircraft; the structure being all-metal with a multi-spar cantilever wing, while the remainder of the fuselage was built with an alloy framework and skinned with corrugated Duralumin. The tailplane was a conventional biplane design, which remained responsive even at very low speeds.

The G38 was originally designed to carry just 13 passengers and five crew plus cargo, but by the time the first prototype flew the aircraft's capacity had risen to 30 passengers. This was made up of an eleven-seat cabin in the fuselage, the remainder seated within the wings and a lucky pair accommodated in a semi-glazed nose.

The only other nation to show an interest in the G38 was Japan, with Mitsubishi building six bomber versions of the aircraft under the designation Ki-20. The aircraft remained in service until the beginning of World War Two.

## Service

The prototype G38, c/n 3301, D-2000 made its maiden flight in the hands of Zimmermann on November 6, 1929. After many months of flight trials, during which time the G38 was purchased by the Reich Air Ministry in March 1930, D-2000 entered service with Lufthansa on May 2, flying the Tempelhof to Croydon route. Prior to this Zimmerman and Schinzinger broke the world 11,025lb payload record on April 10 between Dessau and Leipzig in 3hr 2min at an average speed of 114.5mph. D-2000 was later withdrawn from service for extensive modifications, including a double-decker fuselage which raised the passenger capacity to 34. The aircraft re-emerged with new engines as well and was re-registered as D-AZUR and named *Deutschland*.

On May 14, 1932, a second G38, D-2500 completed its maiden flight, the aircraft being accepted by Lufthansa in July 1932. D-2500 was named *Generalfeldmarschall von Hindenburg* in April 1933 and by March 1934 was re-registered as D-APIS.

D-AZUR was written off at Dessau on May 26, 1936, while D-APIS served on until the beginning of World War Two when it was impressed into the Luftwaffe. After sterling service, the last of the giant G38s was destroyed by the RAF during a raid on Tattoi airfield near Athens on May 17, 1941.

| Technical Data – G38, G38CE and KI-20 | |
| --- | --- |
| ENGINE | Two 640hp Junkers L55 & two 395hp Junkers L8; (ce) four 640hp L55; (20) four supercharged Junkers L88; later four Jumo 204 |
| WINGSPAN | 144ft 4¼in |
| LENGTH | 70ft 4½in |
| HEIGHT | 23ft 8in |
| WING AREA | 3,120sq ft |
| EMPTY WEIGHT | 32,876lb; (ce) 37,044lb; (20) 32,881lb |
| LOADED WEIGHT | 46,823lb; (ce) 52,920lb; (20) 55,941lb |
| MAX SPEED | 118mph; (ce) 124mph |
| CEILING | (ce) 11,808ft |
| RANGE | 1,211 miles; (ce) (max) 3,500 miles |
| ENDURANCE | 5 hours |
| ACCOMMODATION | Seven crew and up to 34 passengers |

An impressive aircraft from any angle, the G38 represented a near 20 year-long dream by Hugo Junkers to see a passenger carrying flying-wing type aircraft in the air. This is the second aircraft, D-2500 *Generalfeldmarschall von Hindenburg*, at Halle. Note the substantial double-bogey undercarriage which was originally semi-enclosed in a pair of large spats.

The original G38, D-AZUR *Deutschland*, shown in service with the clearly 'Reich' controlled Lufthansa. Note the glazed nose where two passengers could be accommodated, presumably at extra charge, to enjoy an incredible view which could not be seen from traditional airliners.

# J52 (Ju 52/1M and K45)

## Development

As with many great classic aircraft over the years, there is usually an unsung hero that paved the way for the development of a better aircraft. This was the case with the famous Ju 52/3m, which was preceded by a single-engined version originally intended as a freight transport.

## Design

The Ju 52, designed by Hugo Junkers and Ernst Zindel, was an all-metal aircraft with a cantilever wing fitted with a full-span aileron and flap system and a skin covered in corrugated Duralumin. The capacious fuselage had 590ft3 of clear cargo space and to aid with the loading of freight the Ju 52 had a 5ft 3in by 4ft 11in hatch positioned on the port side, just aft of the wing. A second hatch, 4ft 11in by 3ft 11¼in, was also located in the roof of the fuselage so that awkward cargoes could be loaded by crane.

Power for the prototype, c/n 4001, was a single 680hp BMW VIIaU radial although the BMW IXU, Rolls Royce Buzzard, Junkers L88, Jumo 4 and Armstrong Siddeley Leopard were also used.

## Service

The prototype, later registered as D-1974, was first flown by Zimmermann on September 3, 1930, and, after flight testing and some fine tuning, the aircraft was delivered to the DVL (Deutsche Verkehrsfliegerschule (German Pilot School) at Berlin-Adlershof on December 6, 1930. The aircraft made its public appearance at Tempelhof on February 17, 1931, and during June and July the Ju 52 conducted trials with Air Express GmbH. During this period D-1974 performed a 3,726-mile-long flight from Budapest to Prague via Bucharest, Sofia, Belgrade, Athens and Vienna.

Re-engined with a Junkers L88 powerplant, D-1974 re-emerged as a Ju 52/1mba and was first flown by Fritz Harder in this form on January 18, 1932. By this time a second Ju 52, c/n 4002, D-2133 had completed its maiden flight with an 800hp Leopard engine. This aircraft was later fitted with floats, first flying as a seaplane from the Elbe on July 17, 1931, with Zimmermann at the controls. The floats used were not successful, but this configuration would be refined and used to better effect on the Ju 52/3m.

As the design evolved Zindel introduced the idea of the Ju 52 carrying up to 17 passengers, but Lufthansa would not allow such an aircraft to enter service with just one engine. As a result, the prototype Ju 52 was trialled with dummy engineless nacelles complete with twin-blade propellers, which would be developed into the famous tri-engined version.

## Production

It was the intention to manufacture twelve Ju 52/1ms but only six were built in the end, the remainder being converted to the three engined Ju 52/3m on the production line. The single engine aircraft were built as c/n 4001 to 4006. Known serials were D-1974 (later D-UZYP), D-2133 (later D-USUS), D-USON, D-2317 (later K45c SE-ADM and D-UBES), D-2356 and CF-ARM. The latter was the only sale of a Ju 52/1 which was delivered to Canadian Airways Ltd (later Canadian Pacific) in 1931. CF-ARM remained in service until 1947 and today a replica of this aircraft is exhibited in the Western Canada Air Museum.

| Technical Data – Ju 52/1MBE | |
|---|---|
| ENGINE | One 680hp BMW VIIaU |
| WINGSPAN | 96ft 9½in |
| LENGTH | 60ft 8¼in |
| WING AREA | 1,249sq ft |
| EMPTY WEIGHT | 8,577lb |
| LOADED WEIGHT | 14,553lb |
| LANDING SPEED | 48mph |
| CRUISING SPEED | 99mph |
| MAX SPEED | 118mph |
| CEILING | 9,184ft |
| RANGE | 621 to 932 miles |
| ACCOMMODATION | Two crew and up to 15 passengers |

*Right*: The only Ju 52/1m to be sold commercially was c/n 4006, CF-ARM, which was delivered to Canadian Airways in 1931 and remained in service until 1947.

*Below*: D-2133 on the River Elbe. It first flew as a seaplane from here on July 17, 1931, with Zimmermann at the controls. The floats, which were 36ft 3in long, were made at Sachsenberg dockyard in Rosslau.

# Ju 52/3M (Civilian)

## Development

The three-engined younger sibling of the Ju 52/1m, designated as the Ju 52/3m was produced in greater numbers in Europe than any other transport type aircraft. An unremarkable design, the Ju 52/3m owes its success to all the rugged Junkers designs that had gone before it, combined with plenty of power in hand.

## Design

The Ju 52/3m differed very little from its single-engined predecessor other than the obvious two extra engines. Other finer changes were revisions to the tail surfaces, a modified fuselage more geared to passenger transport work and an updated cockpit arrangement.

## Service

The fi rst aircraft built as a three-engined machine was c/n 4008 (one of the twelve originally laid down as a Ju 52/1m) which made its maiden flight on March 7, 1932. Later registered as CB-17 *Juan de Valle*, the Ju 52/3mce was the first one sold, going to Lloyd Aereo Boliviano (LAB), the first of four for the airline. All of the airlines' Ju 52/3ms served in both the passenger and transport roles and their versatility shone through as military transports during the Grand Chaco War.

Lufthansa, unsurprisingly, was destined to become the most prolific user of the type and received its first example, D-2201 named *Boelcke*; the second aircraft, which set the tone for being named after German World War One aces, was christened *Richthofen*. Serialled D-2202, this aircraft was delivered in September 1932. Such was the demand Lufthansa had 51 on strength by late 1935, which equated to over 85% of its entire fleet. The Ju 52/3m remained the dominant Lufthansa type until the early stages of World War Two; 78 were credited to Lufthansa on December 31, 1941, all of them still performing the civilian roles of passenger, mail and cargo services. From 1935 to 1939, 230 Ju 52/3ms were actually registered with Lufthansa at one stage or another; a large number of these wore the German carrier's livery whilst being delivered to other operators across the globe or were being employed on development work for Junkers.

Prior to the Ju 52/3m entering service with Lufthansa forced landings were occurring at a rate of 7 incidents per 621,370 miles (1 million km) but following the introduction of the Junkers airliner this was reduced to just 1.5 incidents.

The civilian version of the Ju 52/3m was a colossal success and would have remained so for many more years if World War Two had not intervened. Aircraft were sold to a host of operators across Europe, China, South Africa and South America to name a few. At least 120 were sold to 'non-Lufthansa' operators in Germany alone, however many of these were later transferred to Luftwaffe operated aircraft, an air force that would take full advantage of Junkers latest and most successful design.

The exact number of pure civilian Ju 52 aircraft is not clear, but it cannot be far short of 1,000 of the total of approximately 5,000 built. As a result, several civilian versions are preserved today and of the eight aircraft that remain airworthy, four of them are still earning their keep as commercial aircraft.

| Technical Data – Ju 52/3MG3E | |
|---|---|
| ENGINE | Three 600hp BMW Hornet |
| WINGSPAN | 95ft 11½in |
| LENGTH | 62ft |
| WING AREA | 1,189sq ft |
| EMPTY WEIGHT | 11,785lb |
| LOADED WEIGHT | 20,282lb |
| LANDING SPEED | 60mph |
| CRUISING SPEED | 152mph |
| MAX SPEED | 180mph |
| RANGE | 568 miles |
| ACCOMMODATION | Three crew and 15–17 passengers |

*Right*: The oldest airworthy Ju 52/3m in the original Lufthansa colours of D-AQUI (actually D-CDLH), as it would have appeared circa 1936, over the suburbs of Berlin. The aircraft is operated by Lufthansa and is not to be confused with the CASA 352, also sporting D-AQUI on static display at Sinsheim. (Lufthansa)

*Below*: One of five Ju 52s operated by British Airways, both before and after World War Two, was G-AERU. Bought from ABA Sweden in January 1937, the aircraft was used on the night mail service from London to Stockholm until September 1941 when it was sold to Sabena. (*Aeroplane*)

Ex-Swiss Air Force (A-703) Ju 52/3mg4e HB-HOS has been operated by JU-AIR out of Dübendorf near Zurich since 1983.

JU-AIR
IWC

# J49 (Ju 49)

## Development

Born during a period when Hugo Junkers was being ordered to tighten his belt, the expenditure needed for a high-altitude research aircraft was provided by the DVL (Deutsche Versuchsanstalt fur Lufthart) in 1929. To support high-altitude research the DVL had already set up a specialised Hohenflugstelle (High-Altitude Flight Department) at Berlin-Adlershof in 1926; it was now up to Junkers to design and build a world-beating machine.

## Design

The Ju 49 was a low-wing monoplane covered in corrugated Duralumin skin. The wing had a high aspect ratio complete with double-wing ailerons and inboard flaps while the fin was fitted with a balanced rudder. As variable pitch propellers were yet to be developed, to cope with thin high-altitude air the Ju 49 was fitted with a giant 18ft 4½in diameter four-bladed, broad-chord propeller. The propeller was driven via a long shaft and powered by a Junkers L88 engine, which was a stop gap until the specialist high-altitude L88A was available. The L88A comprised a pair of L8 six-cylinder engines coupled together, and combined with a supercharger gave a healthy 700hp that could be delivered at 19,000ft. To give clearance for the massive propeller the Ju 49 had to be fitted with an unusually long undercarriage fitted with standard Junkers rubber shock absorbers.

The most significant feature of the Ju 49 was the crew's accommodation which was a double-walled pressure cabin, created as a complete module; the first of its kind to be built in Germany. The module was constructed of welded sheet metal, some of it Elektron, and was wrapped in a thermal 'blanket', but the pilot could only see through five small apertures, very similar to portholes in a ship. The design of the module was patented by Hugo Junkers on November 1, 1931. To help the pilot land the aircraft, a periscope was fitted which gave a view from below the aircraft; far from ideal but it seemed to work!

## Service

Two years in the making the prototype, later registered as D-UBAZ, undertook its maiden flight on October 2, 1932, in the hands of Fritz Hoppe. Various technical problems plagued the Ju 49 into 1933, but in September of that year, with the standard L88 engine still in place, the aircraft managed to reach 30,504ft. The engine was duly upgraded in 1934 (redesignated as the Ju 49ba) and, with more horsepower available, the aircraft began to reach the heights where records could be broken. This was achieved on November 1, 1934, when, with an all-up weight of 8,820lb the aircraft reached 41,000ft; a new class world record.

The target was to reach 52,480ft but this could only be achieved with a three-stage supercharger and a variable pitched propeller. Sadly, the aircraft was written off in an accident in 1936 before these could be fitted. However, the research and data gleaned from this project would serve Junkers well with the future EF61 and the Ju 86P.

| Technical Data – Ju 49 | |
|---|---|
| ENGINE | One 788hp Junkers L88a |
| WINGSPAN | 92ft 8¼in |
| LENGTH | 56ft 5¼in |
| WING AREA | 1,054sq ft |
| EMPTY WEIGHT | 7,916lb |
| LOADED WEIGHT | 9,415lb |
| MAX SPEED | (sea level) 91mph |
| MAX SPEED | (at 42,640ft) 137mph |
| CLIMB RATE | 26,240ft in 38min |
| ABSOLUTE CEILING | 42,640ft |
| RANGE | 279 miles |

Ju 49 D-UBAZ after it was fitted with the L88a engine – given away by the single exhaust and the under-fuselage intercooler.

# Ju 60

## Development

When Swissair ordered the American-built Lockheed Orion high-speed airliner, capable of flying at 176mph and travelling a distance of 683 miles, the aircraft was seen as a challenger to Lufthansa and the prestige of Germany as a whole. Only two Orions would be ordered by Swissair, but this still prompted the German Air Ministry to request Junkers and Heinkel to build a competitor. Heinkel set to work on the He 70, capable of 195mph, while Pohlmann produced the EF 30, later designated as the Ju 60, which had the potential to travel at 211mph.

## Design

Several novel ideas were initially incorporated into the Ju 60 including a single main undercarriage first trialled on the A 50, but this was soon replaced by a conventional twin retractable undercarriage. The latter was a forward retracting system but left a large proportion of the wheel exposed which helped in the event of a forced wheels-up landing, although the prototype was destined to fly with a fixed undercarriage. Powerplant layouts ranged from single through to three-engined proposals, the single option proving to be the most efficient. Pohlmann designed the aircraft to have a smooth skin so the promised 200mph plus target could be achieved. However, this was overruled by Lufthansa chairman, Erhard Milch, who preferred the stronger corrugated method which obviously had the disadvantage of a lower top speed. With the decision made, the Ju 60 would become the last Junkers' aircraft to be built with a corrugated skin.

Accommodation was provided for six passengers while the two pilots operated in tandem under a fully enclosed raised cockpit perched behind the BMW Hornet C engine. The powerplant was fully enclosed inside a NACA metal cowling and the BMW drove a three-bladed all metal propeller. A Siemens Sh20 and Pratt & Whitney T2D2 engine was also trialled in the Ju 60V1.

## Service

Work on the Ju 60 was accelerated once the first Orion was delivered to Swissair in May 1932. However, the prototype designated as the Ju 60V1, c/n 4200 and serialled D-5, did not make its maiden flight until November 8, 1932, while the competing He 70V1 flown by Willy Neunhofen, completed its maiden flight on December 1. The performance of the Ju 60 was disappointing andnot helped by the fixed undercarriage; only a maximum speed of 177mph was reached. Lufthansa ordered the Heinkel instead and only a pair of the Junkers aircraft was ever built. Clearly one of the reasons for the poor performance was the wrong choice of aircraft skin due to the intervention of Lufthansa.

Ju 60 c/n 4200 (later re-registered as D-URIM in 1934) did see some service with Lufthansa from 1934, as did the second aircraft, Ju 60V2 D-2400 (later re-registered as D-UPAL in 1934), until August 1936. The latter, which first flew a couple of weeks after the Ju 60 V1, was named *Pfeil* and was used on cargo and passenger carrying routes. Production of a third aircraft was abandoned in favour of its successor, the Ju 160.

| Technical Data – Ju 60 | |
| --- | --- |
| ENGINE | One 600hp BMW Hornet C |
| WINGSPAN | 46ft 11in |
| LENGTH | 38ft 10in |
| WING AREA | 366sq ft |
| EMPTY WEIGHT | 4,498lb |
| LOADED WEIGHT | 6,836lb |
| MAX SPEED | 177mph |
| CRUISING SPEED | 149mph |
| CEILING | 17,056ft |
| RANGE | 621 miles |
| ACCOMMODATION | Two crew and six passengers |

The second of just two Ju 60s built was the V2 prototype, initially registered as D-2400. Re-registered as D-URIM and named *Pfeil*, the aircraft was operated by Lufthansa between 1934 and 1936. (*Aeroplane*)

# Ju 160

## Development

The Ju 160 was basically the production version of the Ju 60 and achieved moderate success with the majority, as was the trend during the 1930s, serving on domestic routes for Lufthansa

## Design

The aircraft featured several structural differences from the Ju 60 including the corrugated skin which was replaced by smooth Duralumin. The shape of the wing was also modified by tapering the leading edge. The cockpit was re-positioned and faired off into the upper forward fuselage directly behind the rear of the 660hp BMW 132A engine; production machines were fitted with a 640hp BMW 132E. The undercarriage was also revised to retract inwards and once up had additional covers which completely concealed the wheel and tyre. All of these improvements gave the Ju 160 a much more streamlined appearance; although there was a 23% weight increase more power was available and, the cruising speed rose by an impressive 45mph above that of the Ju 60.

The prototype featured a deep rudder that extended below the rear fuselage and a tail skid, while production aircraft were fitted with a wider chord rudder that was shorter and a faired tail wheel. Another subtle feature change between prototype and production aircraft was that the latter had its access door rounded off and a slightly modified window fitted into it.

Once in service the aircraft was upgraded to Ju 160D-0 standard which gave the aircraft a larger cockpit and generally better crew comfort.

## Service

The prototype, whose construction began as a Ju 60 but was completed as the Ju 160V1, completed its maiden flight on January 30, 1934. Registered as D-UNOR and named *Luchs*, the aircraft was extensively tested by Deutsche Lufthansa from January 1, 1934, onwards before entering full time service in 1935. The German airline ordered 21 Ju 160s generally for domestic services on the 'Blitz' and 'Lightning' routes to Zurich up to 1941. By then the surviving aircraft were transferred to the Luftwaffe but how heavily they were used, and for how long, is not clear.

As well as Lufthansa, a few examples also served DVL and Weser Flugzeugbau in Germany. Overseas one aircraft, EU-ZVI, served Eurasia while another, J-DAAF, ended up in the hands of the Japanese Navy until it was wrecked in Taiwan. This aircraft may have been the sole example that was delivered to Manshu Koko Yusokabushiki Kaisha (Machurian Airtransport Co., China) in 1937.

Several examples of the Ju 160 also served as freighters with a reduced all-up weight compared to the passenger carrying aircraft

## Production

A total of 47 Ju 160s are believed to have been built with the construction number ranges of c/n 4202 to 4247 and 4292.

| Technical Data – Ju 160A | |
|---|---|
| ENGINE | One 660hp BMW 132A |
| WINGSPAN | 46ft 11in |
| LENGTH | 39ft 4½in |
| WING AREA | 377sq ft |
| WING AREA | (1 & 3) 385sq ft; (2) 380sq ft |
| EMPTY WEIGHT | 5,557lb |
| LOADED WEIGHT | 7,828lb |
| MAX SPEED | 211mph |
| CRUISING SPEED | 196mph |
| CEILING | 17,056ft |
| RANGE | 621 miles |
| ACCOMMODATION | Two crew and six passengers |

*Above*: More aerodynamic and with more power than the Ju 60, the Ju 160 was produced in reasonably healthy numbers; the majority of them seeing service in Germany with Lufthansa.

*Right*: Ju 160D-0 D-UGAZ *Iltis* at Tempelhof in 1938. The D-0 variant had larger cockpit windows and improved comfort for the crew. The aircraft served Lufthansa from 1936 to 1941 followed by service with the Luftwaffe. (*Aeroplane*)

# Ju 52/3M (Military)

## Development

It was not long before the Luftwaffe took a serious interest in the Ju 52/3m, not only as a military transport, but also as an aircraft that could be easily converted into a bomber. As early as 1934 a huge 'initial' order for 1,200 Ju 52s was placed by Germany; less than 10% of them were destined to be used as civilian aircraft, the remainder would serve as part of the massive expansion which the Luftwaffe experienced during the mid-1930s.

## Design

Transforming the Ju 52/3m into a war machine was no easy task for Ernst Zindel and his team who came up against several major problems. The most significant was that the aircraft, unlike the majority of earlier Junkers designs, was never intended to be a bomber. The low-wing main spars of the Ju 52/3m were only 2ft 7½in apart at the point they travelled through the fuselage, which would be the natural balancing point to locate a bomb bay or the bulk of the military load.

The normal method of dropping a bomb was horizontally, but instead a completely new vertical delivery system had to be designed and developed by the Heereswaffenamt (German Weapons Agency) and the RLM. Within a short space of time a vertical rack (known as the Elevmag) was produced which could be fitted between the main spars. Up to eight racks could be carried, each capable of holding eight 551lb or 32 110lb bombs. Dropping from the vertical was less accurate and as a result bombing operations were conducted at low level by the Ju 52 to improve the odds of hitting the target.

## Service

The main military variant, the Ju 52/3mg3e, entered Luftwaffe service in 1934 and despite not being a specialist bombing machine the aircraft formed the backbone of Germany's heavy bomber squadrons from the mid-1930s to the beginning of World War Two.

By April 1935, 405 Ju 52s were in Luftwaffe service the first unit being KG 152 'Hindenberg' followed by KG 153, 154 and 155; the latter three having a combined transport and bombing role.

The Ju 52 first went into action during the Spanish Civil War in July 1936. The aircraft was initially used for transport but later served as bomber. From this point onwards no more Ju 52s were produced as bombers because more dedicated types were being developed. Those that were fitted out for the role were still used to drop ordnance during early raids on Warsaw and as part of the invasion of Poland in September 1939.

For the remainder of the war, the Ju 52 served in the troop transport and paratroop role in every theatre of war. In the former role, the type suffered heavy losses throughout the conflict including two-thirds of a 430-strong force which invaded the Netherlands in May 1940.

## Production

Including the civilian variants, 4,845 Ju 52s were built between 1931 and 1945 in Germany, 1945 to 1947 in France and 1945 to 1952 in Spain. In France, Avions Amiot, which built the type for the Luftwaffe, continued production as the AAC-1 Toucan (415 built) and in Spain CASA built 106 as the 352 and 64 as the 352L.

| Technical Data – Ju 52/3MG3E | |
| --- | --- |
| ENGINE | Three 725hp BMW 132A-3 |
| WINGSPAN | 95ft 11½in |
| LENGTH | 62ft |
| WING AREA | 1,189sq ft |
| EMPTY WEIGHT | 12,612lb |
| LOADED WEIGHT | 20,947lb |
| LANDING SPEED | 63mph |
| CRUISING SPEED | 153mph |
| MAX SPEED | 172mph |
| RANGE | 621 miles |
| ARMAMENT | Two (one dorsal and one in a ventral 'dustbin') 7.92mm MG15 machine guns and eight 551lb or 32 110lb bombs |

Luftwaffe Ju 52s after the successful invasion of Crete which began on May 20, 1941. Approximately 400 German transport aircraft and gliders (towed by Ju 52s) helped to deliver 14,000 paratroops onto the Greek island.

The Ju 52 was adapted for many roles; one of the most successful was a mine-sweeping aircraft. Fitted with a large metal hoop under the fuselage, the aircraft were designated as the Ju 52MS (Minensuch-Staffeln) and were much in demand throughout World War Two.

# Ju 86 (Military)

## Development

The Ju 86 was the first major design placed by the RLM since the departure of Hugo Junkers. The requirement for a twin-engined bomber was also issued to Heinkel, which went on to produce the successful He 111, while the Junkers design had a much less distinguished career. Simultaneously, Lufthansa requested a similar aircraft and as a result Junkers, Heinkel and later Dornier submitted designs for bomber and airliner versions of their aircraft.

## Design

The Ju 86 was a twin-engined, all-metal, stressed-skin, low-wing monoplane. A double-wing was fitted and the braced tailplane had twin fins and rudders. Like the Ju 160 before it, the corrugated skin was now a thing of the past as higher speed could only be achieved by using a smoother surface. The skin was attached to the fuselage's oval formers and main longerons by rivets which created a monocoque structure. Intended power was a pair of Jumo 205 engines but these were not ready in time and the prototype, Ju 86a (V-1) D-AHEH, was fitted with a pair of 550hp Siemens SAM 22 nine-cylinder radial engines for its maiden flight.

## Service

Beating the prototype He 111 into the air by four months, the Ju-86 undertook its first flight from Dessau on November 4, 1934. Early flight trials were unimpressive especially regarding control response and directional stability, both being reported as poor. Military equipment was slowly added during the initial trials including a dorsal gun position and a ventral, retractable 'dustbin'.

A second prototype, Ju 86V-3 D-ALAL, was in the air by January 1935; the aircraft featuring a nose turret and a glazed bomb aimer's position. Both the V-1 and V-3 were later fitted with Jumo 205 engines. Seven pre-production aircraft followed, designated as the Ju 86A-0, the first of these flying in December 1935, and by April 1936 the type was being evaluated by KG 152 'Hindenburg'.

In the meantime, Sweden showed an interest in the bomber; designated as the Ju 86K, the first three aircraft were delivered to Swedish Air Force in December 1936. The 'K' variant mainly differed by having Pratt & Whitney Hornet powerplants. Sweden was so impressed with the aircraft that SAAB later built the bomber under licence.

In Luftwaffe service the Ju 86 saw action with KG 88 'Condor Legion' during the Spanish Civil War, but despite several powerplant changes the German Air Force was not satisfied and it was phased out of service from early 1939. However, several were re-introduced into service at the beginning of the war initially as bombers, but later they were employed only as transports.

A high-altitude reconnaissance version of the aircraft, the Ju86P-1 made its maiden flight in January 1940. It was this aircraft, capable of flying at over 40,000ft, which Britain thought would be built in huge numbers with nothing in the RAF inventory to intercept it. This fortunately never happened, but the type was usefully employed on high-level photographic duties until May 1943 when Allied aircraft were regularly intercepting them.

## Production

Approximately 800 military Ju 86s are believed to have been manufactured including two Ju 86 prototypes which were followed by seven pre-production aircraft. Sweden received 39 aircraft plus

16 built by SAAB and a further order for 40 aircraft built by Junkers. Chile, Manchuria, Portugal, Austria and Hungary all operated the Ju 86; the latter having up to 63 K-2s.

| Technical Data – Ju 86D and P | |
|---|---|
| ENGINE | (D) Two 600hp Junkers Jumo 205C-4; (P) two 1,000hp Jumo 207A |
| WINGSPAN | (D) 73ft 9¾in; (P) 84ft |
| LENGTH | (D) 57ft 9in; (P) 54ft |
| HEIGHT | 16ft 5in |
| WING AREA | (D) 883sq ft; (P) 990sq ft |
| EMPTY WEIGHT | (D) 11,808lb; (P) 14,553lb |
| MAX WEIGHT | (D) 18,081lb; (P) 22,932lb |
| LANDING SPEED | (D) 60mph; (P) 56mph |
| CRUISING SPEED | (D) 171mph at 3,280ft; (P) 161mph at 32,080ft |
| MAX SPEED | (D) 186mph |
| RANGE | (D) 932 miles; (P) 621 miles |
| ARMAMENT | (E) Three MG15 machine guns and two 205lb bombs; (P) one MG17 machine gun and two 205lb bombs |

The second prototype, Ju 86V-3 D-ALAL, which introduced a small forward turret and a lower glazed nose section for a bomb aimer.

Pre-production Ju 86s first arrived with KG 152 in April 1935, but it was not until later in the year that the type fully entered service. By early 1939, the Ju 86 was already being withdrawn from Luftwaffe service but was re-introduced during the early stages of the war and again operationally in the high-altitude 'P' variant.

# Ju 86 (Civilian)

## Development

The civilian version of the Ju 86 was produced alongside the military aircraft, although priority was clearly given to the latter as the airliner did not make its maiden flight until five months later. While the Ju 86 bomber missed out to the He 111 and later the Do 17, the civilian Ju 86 managed to achieve marginally more success, despite it not being a natural contender.

## Design

The airliner prototype, D-ABUK, (c/n 4902) was first flown on April 4, 1935, as a Ju 86bal (V-2) with power provided by a pair of Jumo 205 engines. Devoid of military equipment the fuselage, which was only 4ft 9in across at its widest point, was fitted with ten staggered passenger seats plus a crew of three. The second prototype Ju 86V-4, D-AREV (c/n 4904) *Dresden* (later *Brocken*), followed on August 24, 1935 and by September this aircraft had transferred to Lufthansa for operational trials which came to an end in December. At first, flying characteristics were not ideal, but enlarging the area of the wing by increasing the width of the chord towards the wing tip caused a marked improvement. The modified wing was tested using D-AREV and installed in all production aircraft beginning with the Ju 86B.

The main civilian variant was the Ju 86Z; the Z-1 was powered by the Jumo 205C-4; the Z-2 by BMW 132H1s; the Z-3 by Rolls-Royce Kestrels; the Z-5 by the Pratt & Whitney Hornet and the Z-7 by the Hornet SIE-G.

## Service

The Ju 86 entered commercial service with Swissair in April 1936, the first aircraft being Ju 86B-0, HB-IXI. Not long after, Lufthansa received its first aircraft – D-AHYP *Schneekoppe* – the first of twelve Ju 86s which would serve the airline on 18 routes until 1940 when they were transferred to the Luftwaffe. One Lufthansa machine, D-AXEQ *Bückeburg*, conducted an impressive demonstration by flying from Dessau to Bathurst, Australia on August 22/23, 1936, using just 704 gallons of fuel in the process.

Examples were also sold to AB Aerotransport (Sweden), LAN-Chile (4), Lloyd Aero Bolivia, the Manchurian Aviation Company (20 ordered, 17 received), Swissair (2) and South African Airways, which went on to operate 27 Ju 86s before the outbreak of World War Two. The majority of the latter were impressed into the South African Air Force, several of them seeing action against the Italians in North Africa.

## Production

Approximately 60 civilian Ju 86s were built between 1936 and 1938; a dozen of these served with Lufthansa the remainder were all sold to foreign countries.

| Technical Data – Ju 86D and P | |
| --- | --- |
| **ENGINE** | Two 600hp Jumo 205C |
| **WINGSPAN** | 73ft 10in |
| **LENGTH** | 57ft 2½in |
| **WING AREA** | 883sq ft |
| **EMPTY WEIGHT** | 12,169lb |
| **MAX WEIGHT** | 16,975lb |
| **LANDING SPEED** | 61mph |
| **CRUISING SPEED** | 177mph |
| **MAX SPEED** | 193mph |
| **RANGE** | 1,000 miles |
| **ACCOMMODATION** | Two crew and ten passengers |

*Above*: Junkers Ju 86B-1 D-AKOP *Kismet* was the personal transport aircraft of the company chairman Heinrich Koppenberg. He took charge of Junkers from November 24, 1933, following Hugo Junkers' forced departure by the Nazi Party.

*Right*: Built between 1936 and 1938, and also briefly in Sweden during 1939, approximately 60 civilian Ju 86s were manufactured.

# Ju 87A, B, C and R 'Stuka'

## Development

The story of the famous 'Stuka' (an abbreviation of Sturzkampsflugzeug – dive-bomber) began, for Junkers, in 1928 during the successful trials of the K47. With the death of the K47's designer, Karl Plauth, the concept of a specialist dive-bomber became a low priority, and it was not until Ernst Udet began working for the RLM as an engineer that the idea was revived. Thanks to Udet, the German aircraft industry was invited to tender designs in 1934 for a new dive-bomber; Arado, Blohm & Voss, Heinkel and Junkers all responded.

## Design

Designed by Pohlmann, the Ju 87 'Stuka' was a striking looking aircraft, far from attractive and built for one purpose only; dive bombing. The main feature of the Ju 87 was its inverted gull-wings. At the point of the crank a substantial fixed undercarriage with large fairings was fitted. Airborne, the aircraft gave the impression of being a large bird of prey which, combined with the infamous sirens (nicknamed the 'Trombone of Jericho') that were attached to the starboard undercarriage, added greatly to the terror it would inflict upon enemy troops.

The prototype Ju 87 was powered by a 600hp Rolls-Royce Kestrel engine but later prototypes and the production Ju 87A reverted to the German-made Jumo. The Ju 87 featured a traditional double-wing system, but operational experience showed that the aircraft also needed a complex auto-pilot system to pull the aircraft out of dive should the pilot black out. Designed by Askania, the automatic system took control of the aircraft at the critical point of the dive and recovered the Ju 87 automatically back to normal flight.

The Ju 87A, other than the engine, differed from the prototypes by having a straight leading edge while the Ju 87B featured a more powerful Jumo 211Da, a modified wing and revised undercarriage fairings. The Ju 87C was designed as a dive and torpedo bomber for the Kriegsmarine but was cancelled in favour of the R model. The Ju 87R was a long-range anti-shipping version of the Ju 87B, but like all previous marks the aircraft carried the same single 550lb bomb that swung forward on a frame on release to clear the propeller.

## Service

The prototype Ju 87V-1, c/n 4921, was first flown from Dessau by Willi Neuenhofen on September 17, 1935. Sadly, Neuenhofen and engineer Heinrich Kreft were killed when the aircraft lost its starboard tailplane and crashed at Kleutsch on January 24, 1936. The production Ju 87A-0 was the first to enter Luftwaffe service in 1936 and three were used during the Spanish Civil War for operational trials. The Ju 87B also saw service in Spain as part of the Condor Legion, and with production at a healthy rate more than 700 were in service by the beginning of World War Two.

The 'Stuka' played a major role during the Blitzkriegs of Poland, the Low Countries and France, but the type's vulnerability was heavily exposed during the Battle of Britain. As a result, the majority of Ju 87As and Bs continued their service in the relatively safer skies of North Africa.

# Production

Five Ju 87 prototypes were built, followed by ten pre-production Ju 87A-0s. A further 569 Ju 87A-0s, A-1s and B-2s were built at Dessau before production was transferred to Weser-Flugzeugbau GmbH in Bremen. Production was also undertaken at Weser plants in Delmenhorst, Einswarden, Lemwerder, Nordenham and Templehof. 697 B-1s, 225 B-2s and 972 Ju 87Rs until October 1941.

| Technical Data –Ju 87A-1 and B-2 | |
| --- | --- |
| **ENGINE** | (A) One 640hp Jumo 210C; (B) one 1,210hp Jumo 211Da |
| **WINGSPAN** | 45ft 3¼in |
| **LENGTH** | (A) 35ft 5in; (B) 36ft 4½in |
| **HEIGHT** | (A) 13ft 7in; (B) 12ft 9½in |
| **WING AREA** | (A) 343sq ft; (B) 344sq ft |
| **EMPTY WEIGHT** | (A) 5,005lb; (B) 6,086lb |
| **MAX WEIGHT** | (A) 7,497lb; (B) 9,371lb |
| **LANDING SPEED** | (A) 62mph; (B) 67mph |
| **CRUISING SPEED** | (A) 177mph; (B) 211mph |
| **MAX SPEED** | (A) 198mph; (B) 240mph |
| **RANGE** | (A) 621 miles; (B) 497 miles |
| **ARMAMENT** | (A) Two MG17 and one MG15 machine gun and 551lb in bombs; (B) 661lb in bombs |

Willi Neuenhofen warms through the Kestrel engine of the prototype Ju 98V-1 (c/n 4921) at Dessau in late 1935. Note the original twin-tail layout which failed with tragic consequences for Neuenhofen and Kreft on January 24, 1936.

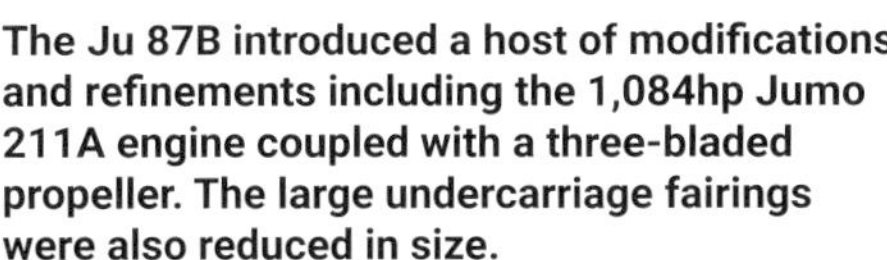

The Ju 87B introduced a host of modifications and refinements including the 1,084hp Jumo 211A engine coupled with a three-bladed propeller. The large undercarriage fairings were also reduced in size.

# Ju 89

## Development

The subject of the Luftwaffe's need for a heavy strategic bomber had rumbled on for quite some time before the RLM first approached Junkers and Dornier in November 1933. The project had the potential to be huge, as orders of up to 400 aircraft were suggested despite the German aircraft industry having nowhere near the capacity to produce such aircraft on a large scale. However, by late 1935 the industry had grown and both Junkers and Dornier accepted the proposal for three prototypes; the former producing the Ju 89 and the latter the Do 19.

## Design

Designed by Zindel, the Ju 89 was comparable in construction terms to the Ju 86 and had similar proportions to the Short Stirling. Colossal strength was achieved by integrally building the wing centre-section into the all-metal un-tapered fuselage which was a monocoque with a rectangular shaped cross-section. The cockpit was set well-forward, and the glazed nose did not compliment the aircrafts appearance, which was finished off by a heavily engineered twin fin and rudder tailplane.

Power was provided by four twelve-cylinder liquid-cooled Jumo 211A engines developing 1,075hp each for the first prototype (V1), while the second (V2) was fitted with four 960hp Daimler-Benz DB600As; both combinations drove all-metal three-bladed propellers.

## Service

The first prototype, Ju 89V-1 (c/n 4911) registered as D-AFIT, made its maiden flight on December 1, 1936, in the hands of Peter Hesselbach. The second prototype, Ju 89V-2 (c/n 4912) D-ALAT, followed on August 12, 1937. Unfortunately for Junkers, the decision to abandon the Ju 89 and Do 19 heavy bombers had already been made before the prototype had flown. The instigator of the proposal for a long-range bomber for the Luftwaffe, Chief of Staff Gen Walther Wever, was killed in an air crash on June 3, 1936, and the idea died with him.

Air exercises in Germany focussed on the issue of fighters and flak defence rather than heavy bombers; future Luftwaffe policy would be to employ lighter, faster bomber aircraft such as the Ju 88 and the He 111.

By 1937, the 'Ural Bomber' project was cancelled completely, although both Ju 89 prototypes were flight tested by Junkers and a potential third prototype was constructed as the Ju 90 instead. Both Ju 89s were taken on charge by the Luftwaffe in October 1938 as troop transports. The aircraft served with LTG 172, D-ALAT until November 1938 and D-AFIT until May 1939.

| Technical Data – Ju 89 V2 | |
| --- | --- |
| ENGINE | Four 960hp Daimler-Benz DB 600A |
| WINGSPAN | 115ft 8½in |
| LENGTH | 86ft 11¼in |
| HEIGHT | 24ft 11½in |
| WING AREA | 1,982sq ft |
| EMPTY WEIGHT | 37,441lb |
| MAX WEIGHT | 61,299lb |
| LANDING SPEED | 68mph |
| MAX SPEED | 242mph at 16,400ft |
| CEILING | 22,690ft |
| RANGE | 1,851 miles |
| CREW | Five |
| ARMAMENT | Two 20mm MG FF cannon and two 7.92mm MG 15 machine guns; a 3,528lb bomb load. |

The second of just two Ju 89s built was D-ALAT (c/n 4912), which first flew on August 12, 1937. As a bomber, the Ju 89 was designed to carry a bomb load of 3,528lb using the same vertical rack system developed for the Ju 52.

# EF 61

## Development

Hugo Junkers had always been enthusiastic about the concept of high-altitude flight for civilian aircraft. Following his departure research did continue, but only with a military application in mind. Building on the experience gained from the Ju 49, work began on a twin-engined high-altitude research aircraft in 1935 which could be developed easily into a bomber or reconnaissance aircraft.

## Design

The new aircraft was designated as the EF 61, the 'EF' standing for Erprobungs-Flugzeug (Experimental Aircraft). The private venture EF 61 was a shoulder-wing monoplane with a round, almost tube-like fuselage. The forward section of the fuselage contained a pressure cabin for the crew, being very similar in design to that fitted in the Ju 49, complete with the same poor visibility portholes. Unconventionally, for Junkers at least, the fuselage was made up of tightly spaced members to keep weight down and was covered in fabric, with the exception of the forward section and engine nacelles where metal was used. The wings had a high aspect ratio and were fitted with split flaps and slotted ailerons. The tail unit was a twin fin and rudder design, the latter being dynamically balanced.

Two 950hp Daimler-Benz DB 600D liquid-cooled in-line engines, modified for high-altitude use and complete with annular radiators, provided the power for the EF 61. These were in place of the intended fit of two Jumo 211 engines but, possibly, a pair of Junkers L88a engines may have been fitted to the prototype briefly after its first flight.

## Service

The first of two prototypes built, c/n 4931 designated as EF 61E-1, undertook its maiden flight from Dessau on March 4, 1937. It is not fully clear to what depth flight trials were conducted although it is possible that the EF 61, on one flight, reached an altitude of 41,000ft before one of its engines failed. However, before testing could be fully explored the aircraft was lost on September 19, 1937, following control-surface flutter which caused the EF 61 to break up. The crew of two successfully bailed out at 11,480ft.

The second aircraft, c/n 4932 designated as EF 61E-2, completed its maiden flight from Dessau on December 18, 1937. This aircraft differed from the first by having a modified pressure cabin, different engine nacelles and a bomb bay capable of carrying four 551lb bombs. It was also completely destroyed in an accident before the year was out, and as a result all further development of the EF 61 was cancelled.

Any thoughts of a high-altitude bomber were put on hold until September 1939 when Junkers presented the Ju 86 as an alternative; the type eventually entering service as the Ju 86P.

| Technical Data – EF 61 | |
|---|---|
| ENGINE | Two 950hp Daimler-Benz DB 600D |
| WINGSPAN | 88ft 7in |
| LENGTH | 47ft 1in |
| HEIGHT | 10ft |
| WING AREA | 700sq ft |
| MAX SPEED | 217mph at 40,852ft |
| RANGE | (projected) 3,728 miles |
| CEILING | 49,213ft |
| ARMAMENT | One MG15 machine gun and 2,025lb in bombs |
| CREW | 2 |

Only two EF 61s were built in 1937, both of them crashing before the year end. The forward part of the fuselage contained the pressure cabin for the crew, the pilot flying the aircraft from the bubble covered aperture on the port side of the fuselage.

# Ju 88A, B, E, and S

## Development

One of the greatest German combat aircraft of all time, the Ju 88 was successful in every role it was asked to serve, from bomber to night fighter and anti-shipping to reconnaissance. Born in 1934 at the same time as the 'Stuka' the RLM at first requested a multi-role aircraft, but realised that this could compromise the whole design, so focus was placed on producing a light or unarmed Schnellbomber instead (as per the Mosquito four years later). It needed to be capable of travelling at over 300mph, able to climb to 22,960ft in 25 minutes and carry a 1,764lb bomb load over a distance of 1,200 miles; Zindel and his experienced design team had the answer.

## Design

The story of this amazing aircraft began with two design projects, one designated as the Ju 85 and the other the Ju 88. The former differed by having a twin fin and rudder tail unit, while the latter had a single fin and rudder. The Ju 88, with construction beginning in May 1936, was a very neat, low-wing, twin-engined monoplane. A crew of three were accommodated well forward under a fully glazed canopy and the lower part of the nose was also glazed although this was expanded to the entire nose on later aircraft. The wing was the most conventional design to date by Junkers, comprising standard ailerons and flaps rather than a double-wing system. Power was provided by a pair of 1,000hp DB 600A liquid-cooled engines, neatly enclosed in streamlined nacelles and cooled by annular radiators.

The initial production variant, the Ju 88A, introduced more powerful engines over two variants and the A-4 had longer-span wings and new bombing equipment. Only a few Ju 88Bs were built featuring a completely redesigned, all-glazed cockpit, which was developed into the Ju 288. The Ju 88E was equally as rare and with BMW 801ML engines evolved into the Ju 188E. The Ju 88S, based on the A-4 series, was designed for speed and the Ju 88S-2 recorded a maximum of 384mph at 32,800ft.

## Service

Originally required by the RLM for August 1935 protracted development did not see the prototype Ju 88V-1, D-AQEN, take to the air until December 21, 1936. Several prototypes followed until in 1939 the first production aircraft began to leave Dessau. Service trials were conducted by Ekdo 88 which took the Ju 88A-1 into action during the Polish campaign. From January 1940 onwards approximately 200 Ju 88s per month were being built and, as a result, the Luftwaffe began rapidly re-equipping, including Kg 30 which saw action in Norway.

The early production machines were involved in both the Battle of France and the Battle of Britain, although losses were beginning to mount during the latter campaign. It was not until late 1940 that the best of the A-series, the A-4 entered service. The Ju 88A was extensively used on the Eastern Front with Kg 1, 51, 76 and 77; although a lack of Ju 87s in theatre saw the Ju 88 being used as a dive bomber, but many were brought down by relentless ground fire. The Ju 88A series was developed further as the torpedo-carrying A-17, but the majority of all versions saw service throughout the entire war. The Ju 88S saw service with the Pathfinder unit KG 66 from early 1944 and with KG 200 until April 1945.

## Production

The Ju 88A was in continuous production from 1939 to 1944, peak production being reached in 1942 when 2,270 were built. Three prototype Ju 88Bs and ten pre-production Ju 88B-0s were built; one Ju 88E-0 and approximately 150 Ju 88S.

| Technical Data – Ju 88A, B, E and S | |
|---|---|
| ENGINE | (A) Two 1,400hp Junkers Jumo 211J; (B) two 1,725hp Jumo 213; (S) two BMW 801G2/G |
| WINGSPAN | (A) 59ft 10½in; (B & S) 65ft 10½in |
| LENGTH | (A) 47ft 1in; (B) 47ft 5in; (S) 48ft 8½in |
| HEIGHT | (A) 17ft 4¾in; (B) 14ft 7¼in; (S) 15ft 8½in |
| WING AREA | (A) 565sq ft; (B & S) 587sq ft |
| EMPTY WEIGHT | (A) 15,986lb; (B) 20,066lb; (S) 18,253lb |
| LOADED WEIGHT | (A) 22,844lb; (B) 27,496lb; (S) 30,407lb |
| MAX SPEED | (A) 229mph at sea level; (B) 335mph; (S) 379mph at 26,240ft |
| RANGE | (A) 934 miles; (B) 1,770 miles |
| CEILING | (A) 30,669ft; (B) 29,684ft; (S) 37,982ft |
| ARMAMENT | (A) Various combinations of MG/FF cannon, MG131 and MG81 machine guns and between 3,100 and 6,600lbs of bombs. |
| CREW | 4 |

The prototype Ju 88, D-AQEN, which was first flown by Karlheinz Kindermann on December 21, 1936.

So many enemy aircraft fell into British hands during World War Two that 1426 Enemy Aircraft Flight was formed to test, operate and demonstrate them to Allied units. The flight flew five different Ju 88s including this one, Ju 88A-4 '4D+DL' (EE205).

# Ju 90

## Development

One of the reasons why the Ju 89 proved to be a failure as a bomber was the lack of powerful engines. This did not deter Ernst Zindel who began redesigning the Ju 89 as a transport aircraft even before the bomber had undertaken its maiden flight. The RLM gave permission for the main components of the stillborn Ju 89V-3 to be used for a new transport aircraft, which was initially designated as the Ju 90S ('S' meaning Schwer – Heavy).

## Design

Using the wings, undercarriage and tail unit of the planned Ju 89V-3 a new capacious fuselage, with a rectangular cross-section and a rounded top, was attached to these components to create the Ju 90. The streamlined fuselage was covered by heavy-gauge smooth-skinned Duralumin, which was flush-riveted to the all-metal structure. The traditional double wing configuration was also used, but with the Ju 90 this was applied, for the first time, to the elevators and rudders.

The 9ft 3½in-wide cabin was huge for pre-war standards, being capable of accommodating 40 passengers in four abreast configuration in five pairs of facing rows; almost like a railway carriage design rather than an airliner. Power for the prototype was four 960hp DB 600s while production aircraft were fitted with the Pratt & Whitney SC3-G Twin Wasp (for SAA) or the BMW 139 (for Lufthansa).

During April 1939 the RLM requested that Junkers should develop two military versions of the Ju 90; one as a transport and the other a bomber. Ju 90V-5 and V-6 were used as the prototypes, redesignated as the Ju 90B. A new increased-span wing was fitted, and power was raised by using four 1,550hp BMW 139s. First flown on December 5, 1939, the V-6 had the novel feature of a loading ramp fitted into a rear fuselage capable of handling small vehicles or bulky freight. The dedicated bomber version, designated as the Ju 90, was not successful and, because of the focus on building the Ju 88 instead, the project was cancelled in 1941.

## Service

The prototype Ju 90V-1, registered D-AALU and named *Der Grosse Dessauer*, was first flown by Hesselbach on August 28, 1937. This aircraft was lost during flutter tests on February 7, 1938, by which time the second aircraft, Ju 90V-2, D-AIVI *Preussen*, had already completed its first flight on December 2, 1937. In May 1938 D-AIVI, powered by four 830hp BMW 132H engines, undertook trials with Lufthansa but despite this aircraft being lost during tropical trials at Bathurst on November 21, 1938, Lufthansa proceeded with an order for eight aircraft. Two others were ordered by South African Airways (SAA), but because the outbreak of World War Two was so close, SAA never received their aircraft and only a few entered commercial service with Lufthansa.

## Production

Nineteen Ju 90s were built, ten as pure civilian aircraft, eight of which were ordered by Lufthansa and two by SAA (ZS-ANG and ZS-ANH). Ju 90V-6 was completed as the Ju 390V-1, while the V-7 and Ju 90A-1 (c/n 0011) were built as Ju 290s. The remainder of Ju 90s were built specifically for Luftwaffe use, the majority for the maritime reconnaissance and bomber role.

| Technical Data – Ju 90 V1 and A-1 | |
| --- | --- |
| ENGINE | (V1) Four 960hp DB600; (A-1) Four 820hp BMW 132H-1 |
| WINGSPAN | 114ft 10¾in |
| LENGTH | 86ft 3½in |
| WING AREA | 1,980sq ft |
| EMPTY WEIGHT | 42,391lb |
| LOADED WEIGHT | 74,264lb |
| LANDING SPEED | 68mph |
| CRUISING SPEED | 199mph at 9,840ft |
| MAX SPEED | 217mph at 8,200ft |
| RANGE | 1,299 miles |
| ACCOMMODATION | Four crew and 38 to 40 passengers |

*Above*: Junkers Ju 90A-1 D-ADFJ *Baden* in Luftwaffe service in 1939, but by March 1940 it was being used by the Luftwaffe with military code 'GF+GA'. Serving with LTS 290, the aircraft took part in the invasion of Norway before being returned to Lufthansa in May 1941. (*Aeroplane*)

*Right*: The first production Ju 90 was A-1 D-ABDG *Württemberg*, which first flew on February 24, 1939. The aircraft served the Luftwaffe from March 1940 with codes 'KH+XC' and 'GF+GB' through to May 1945 when it was one of only two to fall into Allied hands.

# Ju 88C and R

## Development

The Ju 88 was first looked at in the heavy fighter role as early as the autumn of 1938 when the prototype Ju 88V-7, D-ARNC was trialled. The aircraft was found to be a good stable gun platform, but it was not until the spring of 1940, that two more Zerstörer prototypes became available.

## Design

The first examples of the Ju 88C, the C-0 which entered production early 1939 were actually converted A-1s. These entered service as fighter-bombers and were known as the Ju 88Z or Ju 88SA2. The C-0 had a maximum speed of 311mph, which was comparable with the Bf 110C Zerstörer that was entering service at the same time. However, the Ju 88C-0 had a range three times greater than the Messerschmitt which also meant it could remain in station three times longer in the loitering fighter role.

Of the many variants proposed by Junkers, the Ju 88C-2, powered by two 1,200hp Jumo 211B-1 engines was the most prolific. The planned C-1, -3 and -5 were designed for the BMW 801MA which was being prioritised for the Fw 190 instead. The C-2 was armed with one 20mm MG FF cannon and three 7.9mm MG 17 machine guns for an offensive role, plus a single 7.92mm MG 17 in the rear of cockpit and the rear of a ventral gondola. A night fighter version of the C-2 had an additional 20mm MG FF in the front of the gondola. The C-4 and C-6 had a different array of weapons, the majority of an even higher calibre. The C-6 introduced the upward firing 'Schräge Musik' which brought many Allied bomber crews to a quick end. C-4 and C-6 were fitted with radar equipment, but the C-6b was equipped with the highly effective FuG 202 (later 212) Lichtenstein airborne intercept radar given away by an array of Matratze antennas on the nose. The final C-variant was the intruder C-7, the sub-variants ranging from a pure night fighter to the C-7a which carry a 1,103lb bomb load and the C-7b a 3,300lb bomb load.

Based on the C-6 the Ju 88R-1 and R-2 only differed by having two BMW 801MA and BMW 801G1 engines respectively.

## Service

The Ju 88C-0 first entered service in 1939 with KG 30 during the Polish campaign more in a bomber than a fighter role. However, from July 1940 onwards Germany responded to the increasing number of nocturnal Bomber Command raids, by creating a host of night fighter units based across northern Europe. Night intruder units were also formed, the first II./NJG 1 began flying their C-2s across Britain from August 1940. This highly successful unit which brought down many bombers in their own circuits was withdrawn to the Mediterranean in October 1941.

V./KG 40, operating from Bordeaux-Mérignac operated the C-6a day fighter and the C-6b night fighter in a lengthy battle against long-range RAF sorties over the Bay of Biscay to help protect the U-boats and their pens. The route down to Gibraltar, especially by ferry crews, was nicknamed 'Junkers Alley' because of the efforts of V./KG 40.

## Production

The Ju-88C was one of the most important aircraft in the Luftwaffe inventory and as a production reached 3,200 for this variant, with 2,500 built in 1944 alone.

| Technical Data – Ju 88C-6 and R-2 | |
| --- | --- |
| ENGINE | (C-6) Two 1,400hp Junkers Jumo 211J; (R-2) two 1,700hp BMW 801D |
| WINGSPAN | 65ft 10½in |
| LENGTH | (C-6) 46ft 10½in; (R-2) 49ft 1in |
| HEIGHT | (C-6) 15ft 11in; (R-2) 16ft 7½in |
| WING AREA | 587sq ft |
| EMPTY WEIGHT | (C-6) 19,977lb; (R-2) 17,640lb |
| LOADED WEIGHT | (C-6) 27,232lb; (R-2) 25,358lb |
| MAX SPEED | (C-6) 307mph at 17,384; (R-2) 360mph |
| MAX RANGE | (C-6) 1,230 miles; (R-2) 1,863 miles |
| CEILING | (C-6) 32,472ft; (R-2) 30,176ft |
| ARMAMENT | (C-6) Three 7.9mm MG 17 machine guns and one MG FF/M cannon grouped in the nose and a pair of forward firing cannon in a ventral gondola; 'Schräge Musik' comprising a pair of MG FF or MG 151 cannon; (R-2) a single MG 81 or MG 131 in the rear cockpit for defence; offensive armament same as C-6. |
| CREW | 4 |

The famous Ju 88R-1 which apparently defected from its home unit of 10./NJG 3 in Norway on May 9, 1943. The aircraft escorted in by Spitfires to RAF Dyce gave the impression that the aircraft was expected.

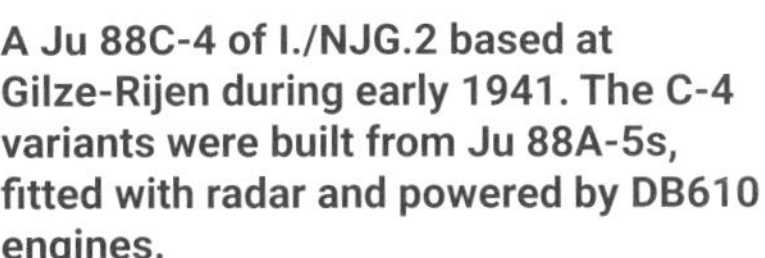

A Ju 88C-4 of I./NJG.2 based at Gilze-Rijen during early 1941. The C-4 variants were built from Ju 88A-5s, fitted with radar and powered by DB610 engines.

# Ju 88D, F, H and T

## Development

By mid-1940 several Ju 88-A1s, fitted with aerial camera equipment, were operating over Britain as part of 121 and 122 Long-Range Reconnaissance Wing. The importance of recce aircraft began to build by 1941 and as a result the first of several specialised Ju 88s, beginning with the D-series, were produced.

## Design

A development of the A-4 and A-5, the Ju 88D carried a similar armament, plus remotely controlled Rb 50/30 and Rb 20/30 cameras, complete with the necessary heating equipment mounted in the rear fuselage. To increase the range of the Ju 88, the forward bomb bay was filled with an extra fuel tank and the dive brake equipment was removed. The Ju 88D-1, which was based on the A-4, was powered by a pair of Jumo 211J-1 engines while the D-2, which derived from the A-5, was powered by two Jumo 211B-2s, 211G-1s or 211H-1s; the latter entering service first. All D-2 variants were fitted with four underwing bomb racks; the inboard ones were designed to carry drop tanks. D-3 and D-4 variants (originally designated as Ju 88D-1/Trop and D-2/Trop respectively) were designed for tropical use, the engines receiving tropical-type filters. A D-5 variant carried a single Rb 50/30 and a pair of Rb 75/30 cameras, the only other modification being a pair of updated propellers. The final D-variant to see service was the high-performance D-6 which was powered by a pair 1,700hp BMW 801D engines. A D-7 version was cancelled in favour of the Ju 188.

A proposed Ju 88F-1 remained just that; the aircraft was to be similar to the Ju 88E-1 but minus the bomb racks. The very-long range Ju 88H-1 only reached the prototype and limited production stage. The H-1 was planned to have a potential range of 2,981 miles with an endurance of up to twelve hours and was developed as a recce and bomber version. The H-1 had a much longer fuselage than previous Ju 88s at 58ft 2¾in so that extra fuel tanks could be carried. Finally, the Ju 88T-1, a derivative if the Ju 88S, was produced in small numbers. The aircraft had the same camera fit as the D-1 and was powered by two BMW 801D engines. The T-2 never left the drawing board but the T-3, a conversion from the S-3, was built.

## Service

The D-variant was first tested using prototype Ju 88V-21, D-ACBO in November 1941. The first production D-1, converted from an A-4, was delivered to E-Stelle Rechlin for trials in April 1941 and by July 1, 350 D-1s and 855 D-1/Trops had been ordered for the Luftwaffe. By early 1942, the majority of the Luftwaffe's recce units and a large number of weather units were equipped with the Ju 88D, serving on all fronts through to early 1944.

The small number of Ju 88Hs built first entered Luftwaffe service in March 1943 and five were on the strength of 3.(F)/123 by March 1944. From May this unit flew very long missions around the whole of Ireland and Great Britain unmolested, until the arrival of the Ju 188.

A few Ju 88Ts, both the T-1 and T-3, saw service with 1./Ob.d.L which carried out regular high-altitude operations over Britain. 122 and 123 recce wings also operated a few Ju 88Ts across Western Europe during 1944.

## Production

A total of 1,350 Ju 88Ds were built, the majority at Dessau between 1941 and 1943, followed by approximately 20 Ju 88Hs and an unknown number of Ju 88Ts, but most likely no more than 20.

| Technical Data – Ju 88D, H and T | |
|---|---|
| ENGINE | (D-2) Two 1,100hp Jumo 211B-2 or 1,180hp Jumo 211G-1s or H1s; (T-1) two 1,700hp BMW 801D |
| WINGSPAN | 65ft 10½in |
| LENGTH | (D) 42ft 2½in; (H) 57ft 10¾in; (T) 48ft 8½in |
| HEIGHT | (D) 16ft 7½in; (T) 15ft 8½in 2,699lb |
| EMPTRY WEIGHT | (D) 18,698lb; (H) 17,640lb |
| LOADED WEIGHT | (D) 25,335lb; (H) 25,137lb; (T) (max) 29,503lb |
| MAX SPEED | (D) 395mph; (H) 242mph; (T) 410mph at 27,880ft |
| RANGE | (D) 1,832 miles; (H) 1,242 miles; (T) (at max speed) 1,987 miles |
| CEILING | (D) 28,208ft; (H) 26,240ft |
| ARMAMENT | (D) Same as the A-4 and A-5; (T) one MG 131 or a pair of MG 81Z in the rear cockpit. ring for observer/gunner in rear cockpit |
| CREW | 4 |

The D model was most numerous of all of the specialised reconnaissance Ju 88s with 1,350 built. The type served on all fronts for the Luftwaffe from early 1941 through to early 1944.

# Ju 322 'Mammut' ('Goliath')

## Development

One of many reasons why Operation *Seelöwe* (*Sea Lion*) failed in 1940 was because the Germans had no large transport gliders capable of landing within a secured landing ground. Under the project name 'Warschau' ('Warsaw'), the RLM requested that Messerschmitt and Junkers begin producing designs for a large transport glider; the former out of tubular steel and the latter out of wood.

Designer Heinrich Hertel and his team at Merseburg set to work immediately on a huge wooden glider under the experimental designation EF 94.

## Design

The basic layout of the glider followed the same theory as the G38 airliner, with most of the payload being carried within the wing. During the early stages of this ambitious design the glider had a capacity for 140 troops and was to be capable of carrying up to 20 tons of cargo including a large range of military vehicles and bulky freight.

The EF 94 originally had a span of 269ft 0¼in but this as reduced to 204ft 6¾in by the time the aircraft was redesignated as the Ju 322 and named 'Mammut'. Considering the Ju 322 was designed for a single operation, the aircraft would be very expensive to produce. Access to the aircraft's capacious hold was via a large curved loading door which hinged upwards. The hold was 36ft 1in wide, 10ft high and 45ft 11in long. Above the centre section of the vast wing was perched a small cockpit for a single pilot. A substantial tail boom extended from the centre-section which supported an angular fin and rudder and a braced tailplane.

## Service

Under the control of a special unit called the Sonderkommando, Merseburg, which was tasked with carrying out the Ju 322 flight trials, the prototype Ju 322V-1 was prepared for its maiden flight on March 12, 1941.

With Hesselbach at the controls the Ju 322 was towed into the air by Ju 90V-7, but it would be a hair-raising flight to say the least. While designed to land on skids the take-off was made on a trolley, but as the giant glider lifted into the air the trolley was late in detaching and was wrecked as it crashed back to earth. Hesselbach experienced severe stability problems, which at one point almost caused the Ju 90 to crash as the glider rose too high behind it. Both aircraft recovered as the tow line was released and the Ju 322 glided back to earth near the village of Blösien. After being recovered to Merseburg, several design changes were made before the second flight took place in April.

On the second flight, three Bf 110s were used but after the same instability problems were experienced again, two of the Messerschmitts crashed before the glider was released. This time the Ju 322 was crash landed back at Merseburg. Further repairs and modifications were carried out and the glider did make a few, slightly more successful flights but in May 1941 the RLM pulled the plug on the project in favour of the Me 323.

| Technical Data – Ju 322 'Mammut' | |
|---|---|
| **ENGINE** | 204ft 6¾in |
| **LENGTH** | 86ft 3½in |
| **HEIGHT** | 37ft |
| **EMPTY WEIGHT** | 64,408lb |
| **LOADED WEIGHT** | 99,688lb |
| GLIDING ANGLE | 1:50 |
| **ARMAMENT** | Three 7.9mm MG 15 machine guns in three upper turrets and potential for two more in beam positions aft of the wing. |
| **CREW** | 1 |
| **POTENTIAL CARGO** | Up to a single Pz.Kpfw.IV plus support personnel, ammunition and fuel. |

**The sole Ju 322 after landing in a field near the village of Blösien on March 12, 1941. It took a pair of Panzers to tow the 'Mammut' back to Merseburg.**

# Ju 288A, B and C

## Development

The long story of the Ju 288 can be traced back to 1937, by which time the Ju 88 had already established itself as the future medium bomber mainstay for the Luftwaffe. Ideas for a replacement for the Ju 88 included the EF 73, complete with a pressurised cabin and remote-control armament which was offered and rejected by the RLM in 1938. By July 1939 the specification that the EF 73 was designed to was revived by the RLM and presented as the 'Bomber B', which would see designs created by Arado, Dornier, Focke-Wulf and Junkers.

## Design

The EF 73 project was overseen by Heinrich Hertel who left Heinkel in May 1939. The early design of the EF 73 was all about speed, the aircraft was aerodynamically clean with a highly loaded wing and a relatively short span, for a bomber, of 51ft 6in. Surface evaporation was used for cooling the engines rather than large radiators and the Jumo 222s or 223s were tightly cowled to further improve the aerodynamics. The fully glazed pressurized cockpit, for a crew of three, was vertically bulged and armament included two remotely controlled barbettes in the dorsal and ventral positions.

Submitted to the RLM the design was tweaked in a few areas, including increasing the wingspan to reduce the loading, before a pair of mock-ups was built in December 1939 and May 1940 respectively. Three Ju 288 prototypes were ordered, the aircraft having evolved into a shoulder-wing twin-engined monoplane covered in smooth stressed skin with an all-metal monocoque construction.

## Service

Flight testing of Ju 288 components began in the spring of 1940 using Ju 88V-2 and V-5 and it was not until November 29, 1940, that Ju 288V-1, D-AACS, took to the air. The V-1 was powered by a pair of BMW 801MA engines as the intended Jumo 222s were still not available. The next three prototypes were all BMW-powered, the V-5 'BG+BU' becoming the first to fly under Jumo 222 power on October 8, 1941.

A demand for a fourth crew member by the RLM saw the abandonment of the Ju 288A, with its slim cockpit in favour of the Ju 288B. The B model also featured a greater wingspan with a higher aspect ratio and modified armament. The prototype four-seat Ju 288B, 'VE+QP', made its maiden flight on May 2, 1942. Unsure of how the development of the Jumo 222 would transpire the RLM's original order to put the aircraft into full production was reduced to just 35 aircraft in November 1942. Engine problems plagued the Ju 288 and various powerplants were trialled resulting in many accidents due to engine failure.

The Ju 288C-1 was to be the production aircraft, powered by the 2,950hp DB 610 engine which would prove as troublesome as its predecessors. The first Daimler-Benz-powered prototype to fly was Ju 288V-101, 'BG+GX', on October 30, 1942. Various C-model prototypes followed, the last of them, Ju 288V-104, on November 13, 1943. However, the entire 'Bomber B' programme had been brought to a close in June 1943.

## Production

A total of 18 Ju 288s were built between 1940 and 1943 made up of seven Ju 288As, seven Ju 288Bs and four Ju 288Cs. The projected Ju 288D and Ju 288G never reached flight stage.

| Technical Data – Ju 288C | |
| --- | --- |
| **ENGINE** | Two 2,950hp Daimler-Benz DB 610 |
| **WINGSPAN** | 74ft 4in |
| **LENGTH** | 59ft 6½in |
| **HEIGHT** | 16ft 4¾in |
| **WING AREA** | 696sq ft |
| **EMPTY WEIGHT** | 29,547lb |
| **LOADED WEIGHT** | 47,165lb |
| **MAX SPEED** | 407mph at 22,300ft |
| **RANGE** | *1,615 miles |
| **CEILING** | *34,112ft |
| **ARMAMENT** | Four 13mm MG 131 machine guns, one 15mm MG 151 or 20mm MG 151/20 cannon. Up to 6,610lb of bombs. |
| **CREW** | 4 |

**Above**: The Jumo 222A-powered prototype Ju 288B (actually Ju 288V-9), 'VE+QP', during 1942.

**Right**: After the 'Bomber B' programme was cancelled, Junkers continued to produce three further prototypes including Ju 288V-103/C1, 'DE+ZZ' which was first flown on August 13, 1943. The bomber was powered by a pair of huge 2,950hp Daimler-Benz DB 610 coupled engines.

# Ju 87D to H and K

## Development

Following the premature withdrawal of the Ju 87 from operations during the Battle of Britain, the Luftwaffe found itself in an awkward position with no replacement insight for their main dive bomber. Fortuitously, Junkers had already set about redesigning the Ju 87 during the spring of 1940 into a more capable aircraft, but this would still change the way the 'Stuka' was taken into action.

## Design

The Ju 87D was a major redesign of the 'Stuka', which centred on the greater power now available via the 1,400hp Jumo 211J engine. The aircraft was aerodynamically improved by placing the oil cooler below the forward fuselage rather than above it and moving the original cumbersome coolant radiator to a position below the wings, inside of the undercarriage. More subtle aerodynamic changes were a refined cockpit canopy that sloped at the rear, neater undercarriage fairings and larger tail surfaces. Defensive armour was improved, and the rear gunner had his fire power doubled to two 7.9mm MG 81Z machine guns. The bomb load also increased to 4,410lbs due to additional underwing hardpoints.

Further variants were the Ju 87F with a Jumo 213 powerplant and the Ju 87G which was the final model to enter operational service. The G model was a specialist anti-tank variant armed with a pair of 37mm Flak 18 cannons supplied with twelve tungsten core shells apiece. The final production aircraft was the Ju 87H fitted with dual controls for flying training. Finally, the Ju 87K represented the limited number export version of which the K-1 was supplied to Japan, K-2 to Hungary, K-3 to Bulgaria and K-4 to Hungary.

## Service

The prototype Ju 87D, D-INRF *Dora*, first flew in February 1941, followed not long after by the first production aircraft, the Ju 87D-1 and the Ju 87D-1/Trop. By the end of 1941 nearly 500 Ju 87Ds were already in Luftwaffe service, the type being extensively used in North Africa and on the Eastern Front. By August 1944 the Ju 87D was being replaced in the ground attack role by the Fw 190 but was never fully removed from the Luftwaffe's inventory as many served on until the final days of the war.

The Ju 87G 'tank buster' was a tricky aircraft to fly but in the hands of an expert such as Hans-Ulrich Rudel, who came up with idea in the first place, the aircraft was lethal. On the first day of the Battle of Kursk, Rudel single-handedly destroyed a column of twelve T-34 tanks; he would finish his career with 519 to his credit. When protected by Fw 190s the Ju 87G was formidable, but they alone could not stem the defeats on the Russian front and by the time of the German withdrawal almost 40% of the 'tank busters' serving in theatre had been destroyed.

## Production

A total of 3,639 Ju 87Ds were built between late 1940 and September 1944 followed by approximately 230 Ju 87Gs; an unknown number of Ju 87Hs, all converted from Ju 87Ds and a total of just 20 export Ju 87Ks.

| Technical Data – Ju 87D-7 | |
|---|---|
| ENGINE | One 1,300hp Junkers Jumo 211J |
| WINGSPAN | 49ft 2½in |
| LENGTH | 37ft 8¾in |
| HEIGHT | 12ft 9½in |
| WING AREA | 362sq ft |
| EMPTY WEIGHT | 7,982lb |
| LOADED WEIGHT | 13,010lb |
| CRUISING SPEED | 186mph at 16,400ft |
| MAX SPEED | 248mph at 15,744ft |
| ARMAMENT | Two 20mm MG 151/20 cannon (one in each wing) and one 7.92mm MG 81 twin machine gun in the rear cockpit; one 3,968lb bomb |
| CREW | 2 |

*Above:* The Ju 87D was a more refined version of the 'Stuka' that went on to be built in greater numbers than all other models. Aerodynamically improved and given more power the Ju 87D was the most successful post-Blitzkrieg version.

*Right:* Another successful and deadly variant of the 'Stuka' was the Hans-Ulrich Rudel-inspired tank busting Ju 87G. Armed with a pair of 37mm Flak 18 cannons, the Ju 87G wreaked havoc against Soviet tanks, but the sheer numbers that the Russians could throw at the Germans would win the day. This Ju 87G is pictured in the hands of Allied troops at Pilsen in Czechoslovakia in May 1945.

# Ju 188A to H and R to T

## Development

'Production without interruption' was the mantra of the RLM and the only way that Junkers could develop the Ju 88 into a bomber, was to do just that. The RLM were convinced that the advanced Ju 288 would fulfil the bomber role but its protracted development resulted in a much improved version of the Ju 88, which was being privately developed in the background.

## Design

The Ju 188 was inspired by the pressurised, bulbous-nosed Ju 88E-0 which performed well at high-altitude thanks to its BMW 801C engines. The Ju 88V-27 appeared next, an aircraft that displayed all of the key features of the Ju 188. The V-27s wing was extended by 6ft 6¾in with pointed wing tips, power was provided by the BMW 801MA and armament included an aerodynamic EDL 131 dorsal turret fitted with a 13mm MG 131 machine gun. A further prototype was produced with a bigger fin and tailplane, which cured the instability problems experienced by earlier aircraft.

The Ju 188A was powered by a pair of 1,776hp Jumo 213A engines and armament was a dorsal turret containing a 20mm MG 151/20 cannon, a fixed forward-firing MG 151/20, a MG 131 in the rear cockpit and a pair of MG 81Z in a ventral position. There was no B model and the C only reached the prototype stage, the aircraft featuring a remotely controlled FLH 15 tail barbette. The Ju 188D, F, H and T were reconnaissance variants.

The Ju 188E, which was the first to enter service, unlike the A model was initially built as a dive bomber complete with an automatic pull-out system as inspired by the Ju 87. Capable of carrying up to 6,615lbs in bombs, the E-2 could also carry a pair of LT F5b torpedoes. Provision was made for a FuG 200 'Hohentwiel' radar in the E and F model, the latter being powered by 1,700hp BMW 801Gs.

The Ju 188G, J, K and L were all projects, while the Ju 188R was a night fighter armed with four 20mm MG 151/20 cannon or two 20mm MK 103 cannon. The aircraft was no better than the Ju 88G and was abandoned, but a few Ju 188S high-altitude bombers were built; this variant, initially unarmed, finally displaying the true ability of the type.

## Service

The Ju 188E first entered service with Erprobungskommando 188 in the summer of 1943, this unit was redesignated as the 4th Staffel, I./KG 66 in August 1943. On August 18, three Ju 188Es went into action for the first time when they bombed the Ruston & Hornsby factory in Lincoln. The reconnaissance Ju 188F followed in September 1943 while the Ju 188A did not appear in then Luftwaffe inventory until early 1944 with I./KG 2 and I./KG 6.

By far the best development of the Ju 88, the Ju 188 displayed very good flying qualities, only marred by impaired vision from its fully glazed cockpit. The aircraft was very popular with its crews, but this did not stop production coming to an end, prematurely in early 1944.

## Production

There were 1,606 Ju 188s built between late 1942 and early 1944; 570 of this total were produced as reconnaissance versions.

| Technical Data – Ju 188E | |
|---|---|
| ENGINE | Two 1,600hp BMW DB 801ML, 801D and 801G |
| WINGSPAN | 72ft 2in |
| LENGTH | 49ft 0½in |
| HEIGHT | 14ft 7¼in |
| WING AREA | 603sq ft |
| EMPTY WEIGHT | 21,763lb |
| NORMAL LOADED WEIGHT | 32,017lb |
| MAX SPEED | 311mph at 19,680ft |
| RANGE | 1,211 miles |
| CEILING | 30,668ft |
| ARMAMENT | (E-2) One EDL dorsal turret with a 13mm MG 131 machine; provision for up 6,615lbs of bombs or two LT 1b or LT F5b torpedoes. |
| CREW | 5 |

*Right*: The definitive Ju 188 prototype, V-44 'NF+KQ', which introduced the final modifications of a bigger fin and tailplane, to improve directional instability.

*Below*: Ju 188V-2 c/n 260151 was converted into the sole Ju 188G-1 variant. The G-1 featured a manually operated rear turret fitted with a pair of MG 131 machine guns. The turret was so small the idea was abandoned.

# Ju 290

## Development

A direct development of the Ju 90, a military version of what would become the Ju 290 was being designed in the background from 1939. Three military prototypes of the Ju 90 were in the air by 1942 and such was the need for large transport aircraft, these machines were immediately pressed into Luftwaffe service to help the isolated Sixth Army fighting at Stalingrad.

## Design

The first production aircraft, compared to the three prototypes, was the first true Ju 290 and the product of three years developmental work. Considering its large proportions and militarisation, the Ju 290 was a good-looking aircraft. The aircraft differed from the Ju 90 in having a dihedral tailplane with more angular end-plate fins and a greater wingspan, fitted with slotted ailerons and flaps. The Ju 290A-1 was fitted with a Trapoklappe rear loading ramp that was 7ft 8in wide and 16ft 2in long, making the carriage of any vehicle up to the size of an SdKfz 251 half-track possible. Power was provided by four 1,600hp BMW 801L radial engines driving wooden three-bladed propellers. Following the experiences of the prototypes over Russia, the production A-1 was well equipped with an array of defensive weapons.

## Service

The prototype was partially built Ju 90A-1 (c/n 0011) which was finished as Ju 290V-1 (c/n 4918) 'BD+TX' and first flown from Dessau on July 16, 1942. This aircraft, along with the V-2 and V-3, helped deliver supplies and retrieve the wounded during the Stalingrad campaign, although the V-1 was tragically lost on January 19, 1943, with 79 soldiers on board when it stalled after take-off.

The Ju 290A-1s left the production line directly into Luftwaffe service, at first with LTS 290. By the spring of 1943 the Fw 200 Condor was beginning to suffer losses and a maritime version of the Ju 290, designated the A-2 and A-3, was selected to take over the long-range role. Despite heavy armament and the ability to fly a lot further than the Fw 200 there were only three Ju 290A-2s and three A-3s. The A-2/3 was equipped with a FuG 200 'Hohentwiel' search radar, additional radio equipment and an extra dorsal turret fitted with a 20mm cannon. The aircraft served with 1./FAGr 5 which was formed at Mont de Marsan on October 15, 1943.

A few A-7 bomber variants were built that were capable of carrying a bomb load of up to 6,615lb on underwing racks and in the internal bomb bay. These potentially formidable machines could also be equipped with three Hs 293 radio-controlled glider bombs or three wire-controlled Hs 294B missiles. The only other variant to leave the drawing board was the A-9 which carried less armament in order to increase the fuel load for very long-range reconnaissance operations.

## Production

Three pre-production prototypes were followed by approximately 27 A-1s, three A-2s (converted from A-1s), three A-3s, four A-4s, 11 A-5s (improved armour), one A-6 (50-seat, Hitler's personal transport), 14 A-7s and two A-9s. Using Ju 290 components, Letov attempted to produce a 48-seat airliner at their Letňany factory called the L290 Orel (Eagle). No sales were achieved.

| Technical Data – Ju 290A-5 | |
|---|---|
| ENGINE | Four 1,700hp BMW 801G/H |
| WINGSPAN | 137ft 9½in |
| LENGTH | 93ft 10in |
| HEIGHT | 22ft 5in |
| WING AREA | 2,210sq ft |
| EMPTY WEIGHT | 52,920lb |
| NORMAL LOADED WEIGHT | 90,504lb |
| MAX LOADED WEIGHT | 99,225lb |
| MAX SPEED | 273mph at 19,680ft |
| RANGE | 3,819 miles |
| CEILING | 29,028ft |
| ARMAMENT | Two 200 MG 151/20 cannon in dorsal turrets; one 20mm MG 151/20 in tail; two MG 151/20 in waist positions and two 13mm MG 131 and one MG 151/20 in a gondola. Up to 6,000lb in stores. |
| CREW | 9 |

*Right*: Several Ju 290s fell into Allied hands at the end of World War Two. One of the most well-known was Ju 290A-7 'PJ+PS' *Alles Kaputt*, which was flown into American hands at Munich on May 6, 1945.

*Below*: Ju 90V-7, originally built as D-APFH. This aircraft became the second prototype Ju 290V-2 and is shown with military codes 'GF+GH' (later 'J4+AH'). It was destroyed in a landing accident in Athens in October 1944.

# Ju 252 and 352 'Herkules'

## Development

In 1938, design study EF 77, for a new transport aircraft, was drafted utilising the best features of the Ju 52/3m. The key feature of the new aircraft would be its smooth skin, which was so effectively used on the Ju 160, whereas a corrugated arrangement had been employed previously on the Ju 52/3m.

## Design

The EF 77 would have three engines, a rearward retracting undercarriage and capacity for 21 passengers. Considerably more aerodynamic than the Ju 52/3m, the new transport's wing had a parallel-chord central section and outer panels that tapered with a slight dihedral. The capacious fuselage had a rectangular cross-section with a round top, the structure of which was created by a number of pierced frames. The EF 77 attempted to please both Lufthansa and the Luftwaffe but was rejected because the RLM deemed the aircraft was no better than the Ju 52/3m.

Junkers redesigned the aircraft, which by now was designated as the Ju 252, by pressurising the fuselage, fitting a new wing and raising capacity to 35 passengers. In September 1939 the whole project was cancelled by the RLM only to be restarted again in 1940.

Due to a shortage of metal a new version of the Ju 252, designated the Ju 352, appeared in 1944 incorporating a great deal of wood; the only sacrifice from the original aircraft was that the fuselage was not pressurised. Similar in dimensions to the Ju 252 but with less power, the Ju 352 featured wooden wings with a fabric skin, a single, rather than double-wheeled undercarriage and a squarer fin and rudder assembly.

## Service

The prototype Ju 252V-1, D-ADCC completed its maiden flight from Dessau in the hands of Joachim Matthies on June 5, 1942. The same year, Lufthansa placed an order for 25 Ju 252s although this was later reduced to twelve, all of them destined to serve the Luftwaffe instead. These aircraft entered Luftwaffe service with LTS 290 (later Transportstaffel 5), based at Berlin-Tempelhof in January 1943. A few Ju 252A-1s served until the end of the war with Transportstaffel 5 and I./KG 200 as well as Junkers, which operated three on experimental work and as engine test-beds.

The Ju 352V-1 was first flown from Fritzlar, once again by Matthies, on August 18, 1943. Erprobungsstaffel 352 (aka 15.TG 4) was the first Luftwaffe unit to receive the Ju 352 in January 1945 and was employed on re-supply operations to East Prussia, Kurland and Schleswig-Holsten. I./KG 200 also operated the Ju 352 on clandestine operations.

## Production

Fifteen Ju 252s were built at Dessau; 43 Ju 352s were built by Junkers at Fritzlar and seven by Letov in Czechoslovakia.

| Technical Data – Ju 252A-1 and 352 | |
|---|---|
| ENGINE | (252) Three 1,390hp Jumo 211F and later, three Jumo 211J; (352) Three 1,000hp BMW-Bramo 323R-2 |
| WINGSPAN | (252) 111ft 10in; (352) 112ft 2½in |
| LENGTH | (252) 82ft 0½in; (352) 79ft 4¾in |
| HEIGHT | (252) 21ft 7¾in; (352) 21ft 8in |
| WING AREA | 1,308sq ft |
| EMPTY WEIGHT | (252) 28,886lb; (352) 27,563lb |
| LOADED WEIGHT | (252) 48,510lb; (352) 43,042lb |
| MAX SPEED | (252) 273mph at 19,680ft; (352) 205mph at 13,120ft |
| MAX RANGE | (252) 4,099 miles; (352) 1,852 miles |
| CEILING | (252) 22,468ft; (352) 19,686ft |
| ARMAMENT | (252A-1) One electrically operated EDL 131 turret with a 13mm MG 131 and a pair of 7.9mm MG 15 on either side of the rear fuselage; (352) one dorsal EDL 131 turret (later replaced by a HD 151/2 turret) fitted with a single 20mm MG 151 cannon. |
| CREW | 3–4 |

**Right**: The prototype Ju 252, D-ADCC, during single engined flight tests from E-Stelle Rechlin in August1942.

**Below**: The prototype JU 352V-1, at Fritzlar south-west of Kassel, prior to its maiden flight by Joachim Matthies on August 18, 1943.

# Ju 88P

## Development

Whilst tackling the Soviets on the Eastern Front, the Wehrmacht had become increasingly dependent on aircraft to deal with the ever-increasing number of enemy tanks and armoured vehicles. The 'Stuka', in particular, had served the Army well and Junkers continued to devise new methods to deal with the armour, including a Ju 88C-4 that was fitted with a Nebelwerfer rocket launcher in 1942. Unofficially designated as the Ju 88N, the idea was not proceeded with, but a more specialist aircraft designed for ground attack, known as the Ju 88P, was put into production.

## Design

The remit for Junkers was to produce an armoured aircraft fitted with an anti-tank gun which was faster than the proven Ju 87G and the Hs 129B. A single Ju 88A-4 (c/n 2047) was taken from the production line and modified with a large ventral fairing containing a 75mm KwK 40 anti-tank gun. Designated as the Ju 88V-52, the aircraft was trialled at the weapons facility at E-Stelle Tarnewitz against captured Soviet tanks. Some modifications were needed but by June 1943 the production variant, the Ju 88P-1, was ready for test flying.

The P-1 was fitted with the same solid nose as the Ju 88C and a 75mm semi-automatic PaK 40L gun, although one member of the crew was still required to load the weapon.

On June 18, 1943, the Ju 88P-2 undertook its maiden flight with a pair of 37mm Flak 38 cannon, again in a ventral fairing. The P-2 never entered production because its performance was no better than the Ju 87G. A single Ju 88P-3 prototype was built which carried more armour than the P-2. The final variant, the Ju 88P-4, was fitted with a single 50mm KwK 39 cannon and a pair of Jumo 211P engines. The P-4 performed well, but again, never entered production.

## Service

Ekdo Ju 88 (PzJ) was formed in August 1943 to trial the Ju 88P from Flensberg, by which time 18 P-1s had been built. Operational trials with KG 3 revealed the P-1 to be too slow and very vulnerable to fighter attack, although the weapon could be jettisoned in such an encounter. Erprobungskommando 25 tried to test the P-1 against USAAF bombers, but performance was so poor the aircraft could barely keep up with the formation. Several Ju 88Ps were used by NSGr 1, 2, 4, 8 and 9 for nocturnal ground attack operations, in an effort to improve the aircraft's chances of survival.

Tests continued until the end of war, trying to marry a heavy calibre weapon with the Ju 88 when it had already been proven that a well-aimed low calibre weapon could knock out the majority of tanks in service at the time. Everything from a U-boat gun to a flamethrower was tested, as well as more refined weapons such as the 55mm MK112 cannon and the Düka 88, the latter being tested in an A-4 in 1944.

## Production

Eighteen Ju 88P-1s were built, a single P-2, one P-3 and the P-4 was converted from the P-2.

| Technical Data – Ju 88P-4 | |
|---|---|
| **ENGINE** | Two 1,400hp Junkers Jumo 211P |
| **WINGSPAN** | 65ft 10½in |
| **LENGTH** | 47ft 2½in |
| **WING AREA** | 587sq ft |
| **EMPTY WEIGHT** | 17,640lb (estimated) |
| **LOADED WEIGHT** | 25,137lb |
| **LANDING SPEED** | 87mph |
| **CRUISING SPEED** | 230mph |
| **MAX SPEED** | 242mph |
| **RANGE** | 1,242 miles |
| **CEILING** | 26,240ft |
| **MAIN ARMAMENT** | (P-1) One 75mm KwK 40 anti-tank gun or a 75mm PaK 40L semi-automatic gun; (P-2 & 3) two 37mm Flak 38 cannon; (P-4) one 50mm KwK 39 cannon. |
| **CREW** | 4 |

More heavily armoured than the Ju-88P-2, only one example of the Ju-88P-3 was built, which, like its predecessor, was armed with two 37mm Flak 38mm cannon mounted inside the large ventral fairing.

# Ju 88G

## Development

As good as the Ju 88C was in the day fighter role, the development of radar equipment and the amount now needed to operate at night proved to a problem in the nocturnal role. The weight of this equipment alone dramatically reduced the performance of the Ju 88C to such a point a new night fighter was developed with more powerful engines.

## Design

During the spring of 1943 the Ju 88V-104 was used as the prototype Ju 88G-1, powered by a pair of 1,700hp BMW 801D engines. The first pre-production aircraft, the Ju 88G-0, had the same fuselage as the Ju 188 and the wings from an A-4. The aircraft was filled with electronic equipment including the FuG 220 'Lichtenstein' SN-2 radar and armament was a devastating six 20mm MG 151 cannon, two mounted in the nose and four in a ventral pack. By the time the G-1 entered service the nose mounted guns had been removed because the muzzle flashes affected the pilot's night vision. The Ju 88G-1 production aircraft differed by having a DL 131 power-operated dorsal turret equipped with one 13mm MG 131 machine gun, while the engines were changed to 801Gs.

The Ju 88G-2 to G-5 did not enter production, but the 1,725hp Jumo 213A-0-powered G-6 did. The production variants were the G-6a and G-6b powered by a pair of BMW 801G engines and the Jumo 213A-powered G-6c combined with VS-111 three-bladed wooden propellers. With improved radar equipment the G-6 aircraft were similar, on the surface, to the G-1.

The final production variant was the Ju 88G-7, which was very similar to the G-6c, the night fighter had the same wings as the Ju 188 and was powered by two 1,750hp Jumo 213 E engines. The G-7a was fitted with a FuG 220 'Lichtenstein' SN-2 radar, the G-7b with the FuG 'Lichtenstein' SN-3 and later the FuG 218 'Neptun VR' while the G-7c operated the FuG 240 'Berlin' N-1a radar. The G-8 and G-9 did not go into production and the G-10 prototype was later employed as the lower component of the 'Mistel 3C'.

## Service

The Ju 88G entered Luftwaffe service in the spring of 1944, the type serving with NJG 1, 2, 3, 4, 5 and 6, I./NJG 7 and I./NJG 100 which effectively represented the bulk of the German night fighter force over Northern Europe. Many Luftwaffe night fighter aces were created flying the Ju 88G including the greatest of them all, Helmut Lent of NJG 3, who chalked up 102 victories before his death in October 1944.

The wayward crew of a Ju 88G-1 of NJG 2 landed at Woodbridge in July 1944, gifting the RAF its SN-2 radar and 'Flensburg' equipment which was using the 'Monica' tail warning radar of Allied bombers to home in on them.

The Ju 88Gs were one of only a few German aircraft still thriving during the final stages of the war, the type even being responsible for the successful resumption of operations over Britain when 22 bombers were shot down near their home airfields in March 1945. However, the aircraft also infamously became the last Luftwaffe aircraft to be shot down on British soil when the tactic was attempted the following night.

## Production

Intended to fully replace the Ju 88C, production of the Ju 88G fell short as only 800 are recorded as entering service.

| Technical Data – Ju 88G-7 | |
|---|---|
| ENGINE | Two 1,750hp Jumo 213E with MW 50 water-methanol injection |
| WINGSPAN | 65ft 10½in |
| LENGTH | 47ft 8½in |
| WING AREA | 587sq ft |
| EMPTY WEIGHT | 19,845lb |
| MAX LOADED WEIGHT | 32,347lb |
| LANDING SPEED | 87mph |
| MAX SPEED | 389mph at 29,782ft |
| CLIMB RATE | 30,176ft in 26.4 minutes |
| ENDURANCE | 3.72hr on economy power at 29,782ft |
| MAIN ARMAMENT | Four 20mm MG 151 cannon in pod under the fuselage |
| CREW | 4 |

The crew of Ju 88G-1 '4R+UR' of 7./NJG 2 must have been mortified when they realised that they had landed in error at Woodbridge in Suffolk on July 13, 1944. The radar and electronic equipment the night fighter contained proved invaluable to the RAF.

# The 'Mistel' (Mistletoe)

## Development

The idea of delivering an unmanned bomber, filled with explosives, direct to the target was first suggested by Junkers' test pilot Siegfried Holzbauer. However, it was the Italians who first attempted the exercise, using radio control equipment to fly a SM 79 against Royal Navy ships off the Algerian coast in August 1942. Let down by the unreliable radio control, the Americans were marginally more successfully with their 'Aphrodite' project, which involved the crew bailing out of a B-17 before a mother ship guided it remotely towards the target.

The Germans would come up with a much more practical idea, thanks to the efforts of the DFS (Deutsches Forschunginstitut für Segelflug), Junkers and a few hundred surplus Ju 88s.

## Design

From January 1942 serious development of the 'Mistel' project began, focussing on the idea of a parasite fighter with a single pilot controlling the bomber it was attached to. The problem of devising a method of connecting and disconnecting the two aircraft was solved by DFS while Junkers and Patin developed a reliable guidance and control system. Progress was swift as the first 'Mistel' prototype, made up of a Ju 88A-4 and Bf 109F-4, made its maiden flight in October 1943.

Under the weapons code name 'Beethoven' a great deal of modification work was carried out on the Ju 88 to turn it into a 'Mistel'. All unnecessary internal equipment such as armour, armament, air brakes, radio and bomb sight were stripped out while the fuselage was strengthened with extra skin and stringers. Each bomber was also fitted with new engines and extra fuel tanks while the cockpit was reattached with quick release bolts, so that when the aircraft was flown to a forward airfield, it could be quickly replaced by a hollow-charge warhead. The latter consisted of a 7,718lb warhead filled with 3,804lb of high explosives in place of the entire forward fuselage. At this point the entire combination was controlled by the parasite pilot.

## Service

The 'Mistel' first went into action with 2./KG 101 from St Dizier against Allied shipping in the Seine Bay on June 24/25, 1944. Four ships were hit, but several others had to be jettisoned before a target could be found. Further shipping attacks took place on August 9/10 without success. 2./KG 101 were then redesignated as III./KG 66 and moved to Denmark in preparation for operations against the Royal Navy in Scapa Flow. Five 'Mistel' set out in October 1944, but three crashed en route and two failed to find a target before being jettisoned.

'Mistels' were also heavily employed as part of Operation *Iron Hammer* from February 1945 in an attempt to stem the Russian invasion. Some success was achieved against bridges during April 1945, but the majority of 'Mistel' combinations were either shot down before they reached their target because of a lack of manoeuvrability, or they simply crashed.

## Production

At least 85 'Mistels' were 'built' from early 1944 through to the end of the war, the most common being the S1 which combined a Ju 88A-4 and an Fw 190A-6. 125 'Mistel' 2 were ordered in December 1944 and more than 80 were available for use by March 1945; 50 of these were captured by the Allies at the end of the war.

| Technical Data – Mistel Junkers Combinations | |
| --- | --- |
| **DESIGNATION** | Mistel 1 to 6 |
| **AIRCRAFT** | (1 & S1) Ju88A-4/Bf109F-4; (2) Ju88G-1/Fw190A-6; (3A) Ju88G-10/Fw190F-8; (3B, 3C & 3D**) Ju88H-4/Fw190A-8; (4) Ju188/Me262 or Ju287/Me262A; (5) Ju88G-7/Ta152H and (6) Ju268/He162 or Me262** |
| **WARHEAD** | (1 & 2) 1,725kg; (3A) 1,000kg; (3B) 1,500kg; (3C) 2,500kg and (3D) 3,500kg |
| **CRUISING** | *270mph |
| **IMPACT SPEED** | *370mph (explosive component) |
| **RADIUS OF ACTION** | *480 miles (fuel carried in lower component for outward journey; 66-gallon auxiliary drop tank on upper unit) |
| *Average across all Mistel variants<br>**Mistel 4 & 6 were proposed; 5 was tested only | |

The 'Mistel' 1 combination comprised a Ju 88A-4, heavily modified with a 7,718lb warhead filled with 3,804lb of HE, controlled by a Bf 109F-4. Once the 'Mistel' arrived near its target, the pilot of the Bf 109 aimed the Ju 88 and, three seconds after release, it automatically armed itself.

# Ju 390

## Development

Even before the United States entered World War Two in December 1941, thought had been given to designing and building a bomber capable of traversing the Atlantic. Once the US was involved in the conflict, the concept of such an aircraft was rejuvenated, and in early 1942 a Junkers' design for a six-engined, very long-range bomber was submitted in competition with the Focke Wulf Ta 400 and the Messerschmitt Me 264 to the RLM.

## Design

Designed in the Junkers' offices in Prague the new, giant aircraft was designated as the Ju 390 and prototype bomber, maritime reconnaissance and transport versions were planned. The aircraft would make full use of Ju 290 components which would shorten both development and production time. The Ju 390V-1 was to be the transport prototype, utilising the fuselage of a Ju 290A, lengthened by 8ft 0¾in by inserting an extra section aft of the wing. The wingspan was increased by 27ft 3½in which gave sufficient room to mount six 1,700hp BMW 801D radial engines. The four inner engines had extended nacelles to house the four main undercarriage legs inside once retracted; each leg had twin wheels. During lightly loaded operations only the inner pair of undercarriage legs was used.

## Service

The prototype Ju 390V-1, 'GH+UK', completed its maiden flight from Dessau on October 21, 1943. Capable of carrying up to a 22,050lb payload, the Ju 390 could carry enough fuel (7,479-gallons) to fly for 4,968 miles or remain airborne for 24 hours. The aircraft became known as the 'Amerika Bomber' because of reports that it came close to the American coast during a test flight over the Atlantic, which was possible, but proved to be untrue.

The second prototype Ju 390V-2, 'RC+DA', was an even bigger aircraft, its fuselage was 102ft 0¼in and the wingspan was increased to 110ft 2¾in. The aircraft was fully equipped for maritime reconnaissance complete with FuG 200 'Hohentwiel' and a similar cannon armament to the Ju 290. However, the whole programme was brought to a close in July 1944 and the Ju 390V-2 was destined never to fly. As a result, the bomber version – the Ju 390V-3 – was never built. It is not clear how much flying the prototype undertook but it remained extant until it was scrapped in April 1945.

| Technical Data – Ju 390A-1 | |
|---|---|
| ENGINE | Six 1,700hp BMW 801D |
| WINGSPAN | 165ft 1in |
| LENGTH | 101ft 10¾in |
| WING AREA | 2,734sq ft |
| EMPTY WEIGHT | 81,585lb |
| MAX LOADED WEIGHT | 148,838lb |
| LANDING SPEED | 87mph |
| CRUISING SPEED | 215mph |
| MAX SPEED | 311mph at 19,680ft |
| ENDURANCE | 24 hours |
| RANGE | (recce) 6,210 miles |
| MAIN ARMAMENT | Similar to Ju290. |
| CREW | 10 |

A remarkable aircraft, just from the technological achievement alone, only one of the three prototypes took to the air. The Ju 390V-1, the transport version of the type, is pictured during flight trials.

# Ju 388J to M 'Störtebeker'

## Development

The Ju 188 not only effectively served to fill the gap created by the failed Ju 288 but would also be developed into a new high-altitude variant, redesignated as the Ju 388. Three variants of the Ju 188 were chosen for the development of the new aircraft, which it was hoped would be able to operate comfortably at almost 40,000ft, a height where they would be reasonably immune from enemy fighters.

## Design

Developed from the Ju 188J, K and L, the new aircraft was simply redesignated as the Ju 388J, K and L. The Ju 388K and L were very similar to the Ju 188S and T complete with a fully pressurised, glazed bulbous cockpit. The Ju 388J was fitted with a new pressurised cabin modified with a metal nose so that it could be fitted with the antennae of a FuG 220 'Lichtenstein' SN-2 radar.

All Ju 388s were fitted with a remote control FLH 15 tail barbette with a pair of 13mm MG 131 machine guns which was only line of defence for the Ju 388K and Ju 388L, designed as bomber and reconnaissance variants respectively. Power was intended to be from the Jumo 213 but these were diverted to the Fw 190D instead and the Ju 388 had to make do with a pair of 1,800hp BMW 801TJ air-cooled radials.

The final variant was the Ju 388M, which was similar to the Ju 388K but was designed to carry a LT 10 winged torpedo. Several Ju 388Ms were being built when the war ended, but none took to the air.

## Service

Converted from a Ju 188F-1, the prototype Ju 388V-1 (completed as the first Ju 388L) 'DW+YY' made its maiden flight on December 22, 1943. By January 1944 the Ju 388V-3 (the bomber Ju 388K) was in the air which was followed by the Ju 388V-2, the prototype of the night fighter Ju 388J 'Störtebeker' (a 15th Century German Pirate). Built from Ju 188S-1 airframes, the first aircraft to enter service was the Ju 388L-0, delivered to Erprobungskommando 388 in August 1944. Only the Ju 388L was destined to enter Luftwaffe service, albeit in small numbers and not fully operational with 3./Versuchsverband Ob.d.L, from late 1944 through to the end of the war. Tasked with carrying out reconnaissance operations over Britain, one Ju 388 flying at 44,291ft over the English Channel was shot down by a Spitfire – possibly the highest successful interception of the entire war. A least four Ju 388Js saw brief operational trial service with NJG 2 during the last few weeks of the war.

## Production

Over a 100 Ju 388s were built but the exact total is difficult to pin down. Six prototypes were constructed followed by 20 Ju 388L-0s, 10 K-0s, a single K-1 and over 60 L-1s.

| Technical Data – Ju 388J-1 | |
|---|---|
| **ENGINE** | Two 1,800hp BMW 801TJ |
| **WINGSPAN** | 72ft 2in |
| **LENGTH** | 49ft 0½in |
| **WING AREA** | 609sq ft |
| **EMPTY WEIGHT** | 23,296lb |
| **LOADED WEIGHT** | 30,352lb |
| **MAX SPEED** | 360mph at 39,360ft |
| **CLIMB RATE** | 1,246 ft/min |
| **CEILING** | 42,640ft |
| **RANGE** | 1,242 miles |
| **MAIN ARMAMENT** | A pair of 20mm MG 151/20 cannon and two MK 103 or MK 108 cannons, all fixed forward-firing in a underfuselage pod and two 13mm MG 131 machine-guns in a 'Hecklafette' tail barbette. |
| **CREW** | 3 |

*Above*: Carrying Foreign Evaluation number FE4010 gives this aircraft away as Ju 388L-1, in US hands at Freeman Field.

*Right*: The bomber prototype Ju 388V-3 first flew in January 1944. The large ventral wooden fairing under the Ju 388K contained a bomb load of up to 9,840lb.

# Ju 287 and EF 131

## Development

Junkers were already at the forefront of turbojet production in Germany but had only ever studied jet-powered designs of their own. However, in 1942 the RLM approached the company with a new project for a multi-engined bomber.

## Design

The research project was led by Professor Heinrich Hertel who recruited the skills of Dr Hans Wocke as project engineer. The design would be for an aircraft capable of Mach 0.80 and powered by four turbojet engines with a swept wing. Later wind tunnel tests did not favour the swept wing design and, instead, a swept-forward wing was trialled by Wocke and Philipp von Doepp. The swept-forward wing was confirmed in further wind tunnel tests as the best option, by which time the project was designated as the EF 122.

In March 1944 a prototype was ordered by the RLM under the designation Ju 287 and detailed design work was conducted by Ernst Zindel and Fritz Freytag. Because the wing of the aircraft was so advanced it was decided to flight test it by using major components from existing aircraft. The fuselage was from a He 177A; the fin, rudder and tailplane were from a Ju 188G-2; the main wheels were taken from a Ju 352A-1 and the twin nose wheel undercarriage legs were liberated from a downed USAAF B-24. The tricycle undercarriage was fixed and the wheels were virtually enclosed by a set of large spats. Power was provided by four 1,980lb Junkers 109-004 turbojets; two of them were attached to either side of the forward fuselage and the other pair, under the trailing edge of the wing.

## Service

On August 16, 1944, a mere five months after detailed design work commenced, Siegfried Holzbaur climbed aboard the Ju 287V-1, 'RS+RA' to conduct the maiden flight from Brandis near Leipzig. Dessau's runway was too short to risk such a valuable prototype and even at the Luftwaffe's test centre a trio of 2,205lb reusable rocket units were fitted to ensure the aircraft took off safely. After taking off in just one third of the runway's length, Holzbaur jettisoned the rocket units, which landed by parachute. Although Holzbaur enjoyed a generally smooth flight, the forward-swept wing revealed its disadvantages. All these problems could be resolved by re-positioning the under-wing engines in front of the leading edge of the wing.

This would be the main feature of the Ju 287V-2 which had six BMW 109-003A-1 turbojets, clustered in threes mounted much further forward than the V-1. Built in a dispersed factory near Brandis, construction of the V-3 began simultaneously. However, in July 1944 the RLM had already abandoned the idea of jet bombers, but Junkers continued development in secret.

In April 1945 all three Ju 287s were in Soviet hands and making full use of the plethora of engineers they had captured, the V-2 was completed and flown not long after. A new project, the EF 131, which was a three-seat jet bomber was also completed under Soviet control from the components of the unfinished V-3. Before the EF 131 was completed, the Soviets moved the entire Junkers operation, which included 500 engineers to the USSR in September 1946.

On May 23, 1947, the EF 131 was flown by German pilot Paul Junge and flight testing continued until at least June 1948. From all this work stemmed the unsuccessful Baade 152 airliner while Hans Wocke, sticking with his theories of forward-swept wings, went on to design the HFB 320 Hansajet.

| Technical Data – Ju 287 | |
| --- | --- |
| ENGINE | (V-1) Four 1,980lb Junkers 109-004 turbojets |
| WINGSPAN | 65ft 11¾in |
| LENGTH | 61ft 0¼in |
| WING AREA | 628sq ft |
| EMPTY WEIGHT | 26,278lba |
| MAX LOADED WEIGHT | (inc. bomb load) 47,450lb |
| MAX SPEED | (without bomb load) 537mph at 16,400ft |
| INITIAL CLIMB RATE | 2,887ft/min |
| CEILING | 39,360ft |
| RANGE | (with full bomb load) 985 miles |
| MAIN ARMAMENT | (V-3) A remotely controlled tail barbette and up to 8,820lb in bombs |
| CREW | 3 |

*Right*: The prototype Ju 287V-1, 'RS+RA', at Brandis near Leipzig. The aircraft was built at Dessau but was dismantled and transported the 55 miles to Brandis by road because Dessau's runway was thought to be too short.

*Below*: The Ju 287V-1 at Brandis, prior to its maiden flight, on August 16, 1944. For this flight three 2,205lb Walter 109-501 reusable rocket motors were attached under each wing-mounted engine and under the starboard forward turbojet.

# Drawing Board

## The Early Projects

Hugo Junkers spent vast sums of time and money on research and development, to such an extent he was often criticised for not producing enough sellable practical aircraft. While his construction techniques were revolutionary, Junkers' approach to aircraft was not conducive to massed production. Early aircraft that were destined not to leave the drawing board were the J 3 monoplane, the J 5 monoplane scout with a pusher engine and the J 6 scout. Another military machine that would not make it was the 114ft 10in-span RI-57/17. This thick-winged monoplane bomber was to be powered by a pair of 256hp Mercedes D IVb engines but was cancelled in 1918. The RI-57/17 (later refined into the RI-58/18) was followed by the 'G-Eindecker' flying boat for the German Navy in November 1917. With a comparatively reserved wingspan of 98ft 5in the 'G-Eindecker' was following by Junkers most ambitious project to date, the colossal 262ft 6in-span 'Flugboot-F'. Again intended for the German Navy, the 'Flugboot-F' was designed to have four 1,000hp engines buried within the leading edge of the wing. However, engines of such power were not available in 1918 and the idea was dropped. Over a decade later the Dornier Do X flying boat bore an uncanny resemblance.

## Inter-war dreams

Junkers main focus, which seemed not be disrupted by the need for war machines during World War One, was the concept of the giant high payload flying wing. In 1920 construction began of the J14 (JG1) with a span of 123ft 4in, but Allied Commission restrictions saw the project scrapped long before completion. Another giant flying-boat design followed in the shape of the 'Junkerissime' which spanned 206ft. In 1924 the J1000, a huge flying-wing, was designed to carry up to 80 passengers and eight crew. Intended for operations across the Atlantic, the aircraft's accommodation was in the wing with power provided by four 985hp engines. All of Hugo Junkers' flying-wing dreams were eventually realised in the comparatively modest G38.

Other inter-war projects were the J28, a two-seat version of the T21; the J44 which was an A35 replacement; the proposed J56 to replace the K16 and the J58 which was intended to replace both the F13 and the W34.

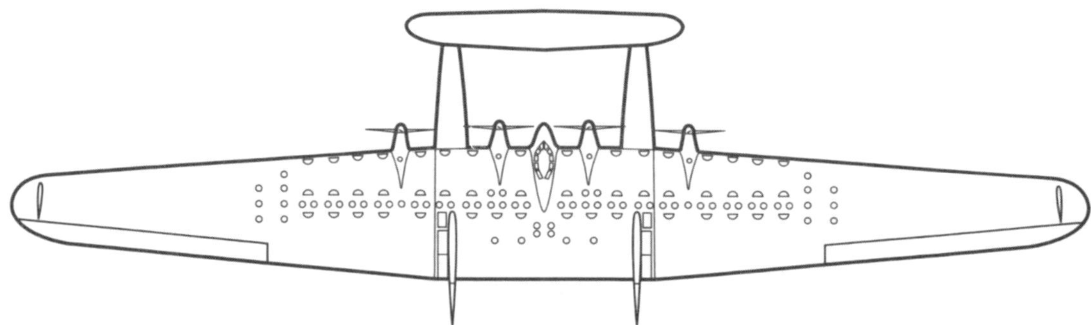

The incredible Junkers J1000 flying-wing with its span of 262ft 6in was a typical Hugo Junkers vision for the future of airline travel.

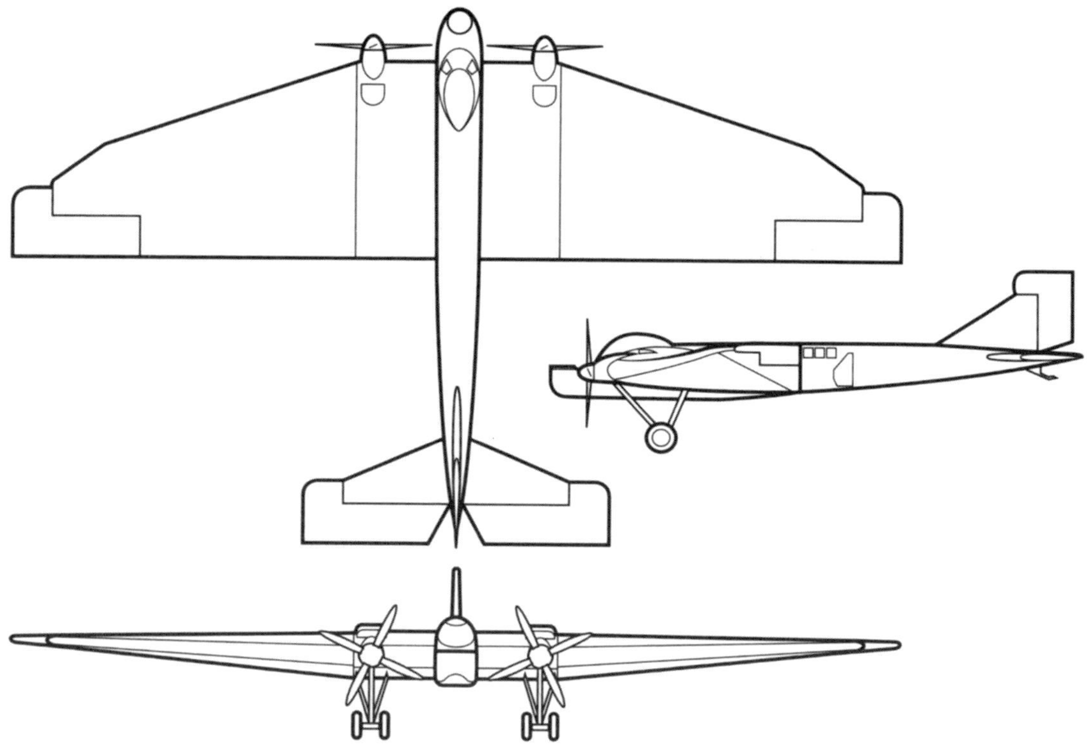

**By 1917, Junkers had demonstrated that aircraft could be made from metal and the RI-57/17 was the company's first attempt to design a large bomber.**

## The 'Wunderwaffen' (Wonder Weapons)

Even during the early stages of World War Two, Junkers continued to design long-range passenger-carrying aircraft including the EF 100. Powered by six 2,200hp Jumo 223 engines, the EF 100 was designed to travel 5,589 miles non-stop with a 44,100lb payload. Cancelled by 1942 the less conventional EF 101 followed. This 230ft, four-engined high-altitude reconnaissance aircraft had a potential range of over 10,000 miles. Powered by four 3,800hp Daimler-Benz engines, the EF 101 was designed to carry a single 'parasite' Bf109 which was released to carry out the reconnaissance mission and then recovered in flight.

There were numerous high-altitude developments of existing aircraft including the Ju 186 and Ju 286, both versions of the Ju 86. A Ju 87 replacement was also penned in the shape of the Ju 187 which was designed as a close support aircraft but only ever reached the mock-up stage.

Another major project was the Ju 290Z which involved joining a pair of Ju 290s together by using a new centre section and creating a machine with a 196ft 10in wingspan. Designed to be used as a transport, glider tug or in the long-range reconnaissance role the Ju 290Z was also potentially capable of carrying its own 'parasite' fighter. The idea never left the drawing board, but Heinkel proved the concept successful by producing their own conjoined He 111Z.

From 1938 onwards Junkers had been working on a number of jet-powered designs to such a degree, two special departments were created, one working on fighter designs and the other

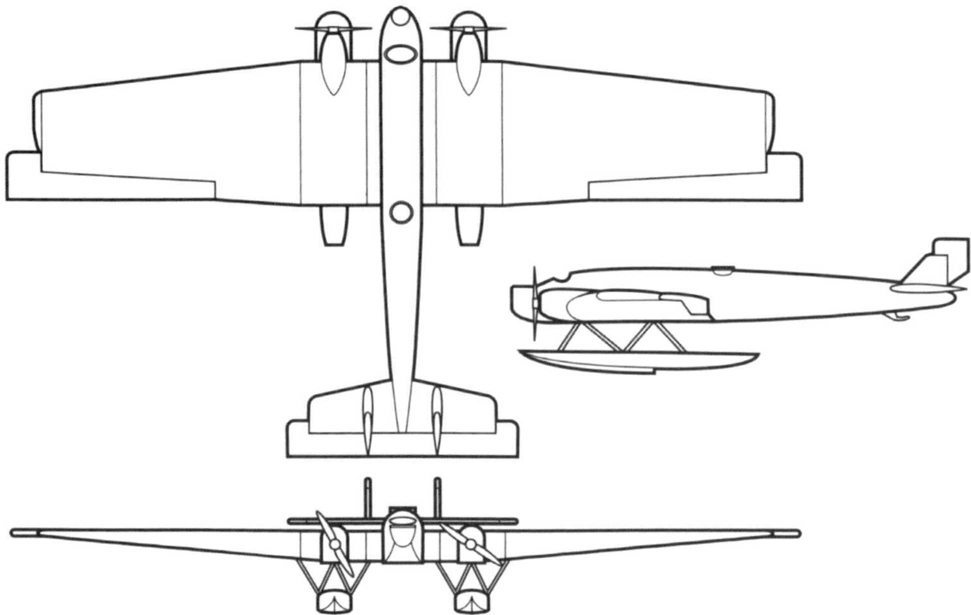

Three prototypes of the 'G-Eindecker' where ordered, but Junkers did not begin construction until data had been assessed from the much smaller J11 float-plane by which time the war was over and the German Navy cancelled the order.

Very different from earlier Junkers' designs, the giant 'Flugboot-F' had a 262ft 6in wing mounted as a parasol above the fuselage and, large extended sponsons that look like small wings. The latter feature, in particular, was incorporated into the design of the Dornier Do X.

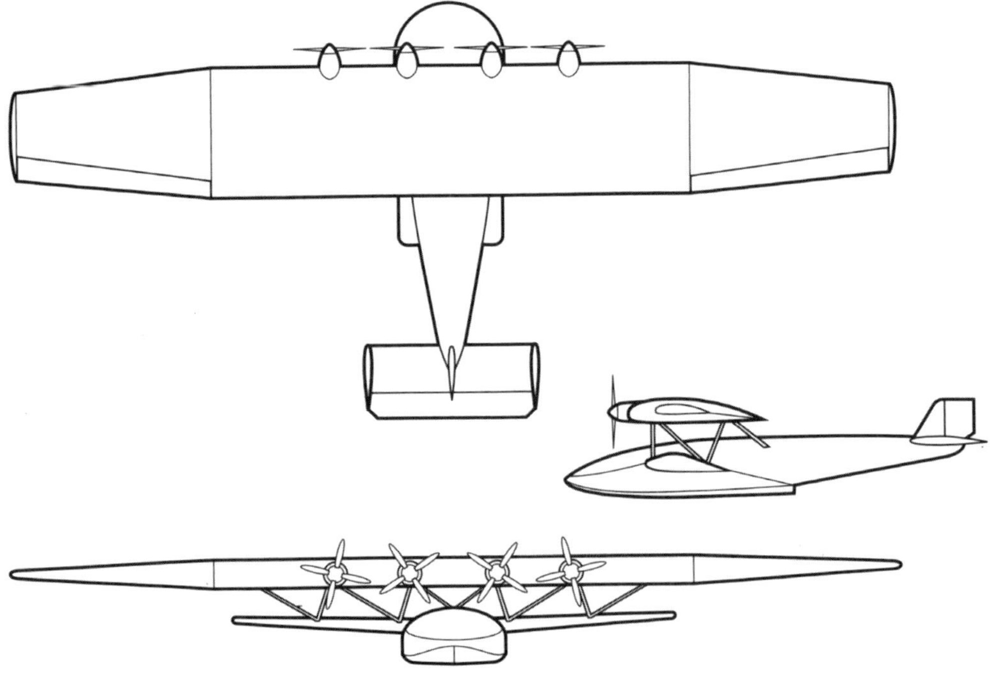

on bombers. Early known projects were designated EFo 008 to 022, the majority of these designs were based on conventional and contemporary piston machines. The exception in this early group was the EFo 009 Hubjäger (Luft-Fighter) which would not have been out of place in the hands of Buck Rodgers. This machine was designed to take off vertically and like all early jets of the period would have had a very short endurance. Several Junkers' jet projects did materialise into working prototypes in post-war Russia, such as the EF 126, a pulse-jet fighter and EF 140 bomber with forward swept wings.

Junkers was no different to any other aircraft manufacturer in the number of its designs which never left the drawing board. However, the majority of its failed projects never materialised because the airframes were so far ahead of the power plants needed to get them off the ground. The scale of some of the early machines was really in the realms of fantasy, but Junkers could never be criticised for not looking forward. If the company had fallen to the Allies at the end of World War Two there is no reason why this visionary manufacturer could not have been designing advanced aircraft today.

**An artist's impression of the remarkable Junkers J1000 designed by Ernst Zindel, which had the potential to perform transatlantic passenger services in the 1920s.**

**Another Junkers giant that never left the drawing board was the EF 100 six-engine very long-range airliner/ transport aircraft.**

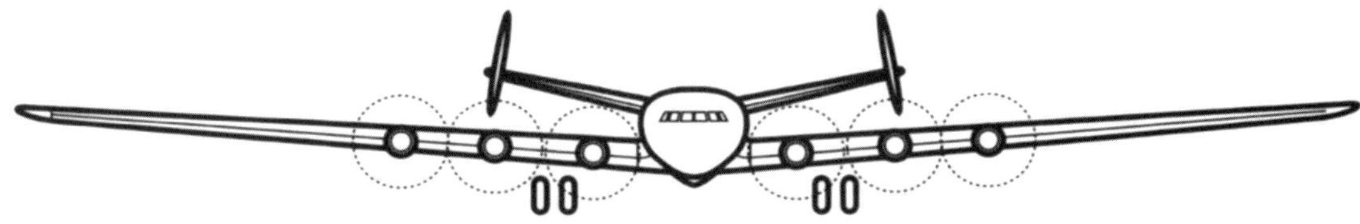

The EFo 009 Hubjäger interceptor, like so many other Junkers jet projects, never went beyond the wind-tunnel stage of development.

Although this arrangement, designated as the Ju 290Z, seems a rather wild idea the concept was plausible and achievable as proved by Heinkel which produced and successfully flew its own version – the He 111Z.

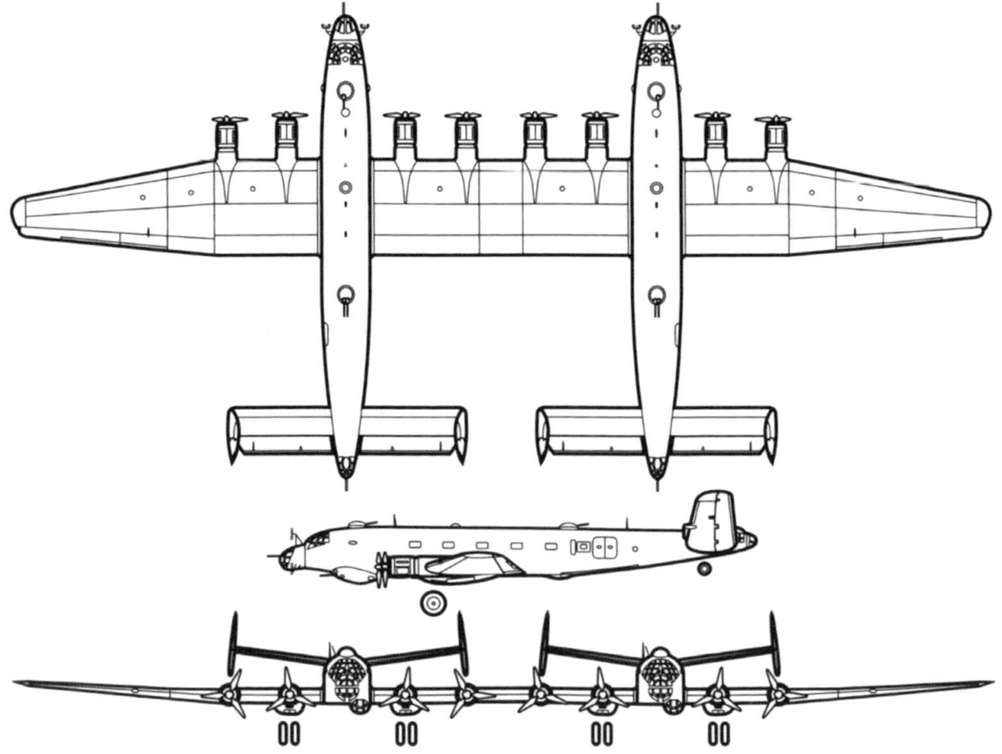

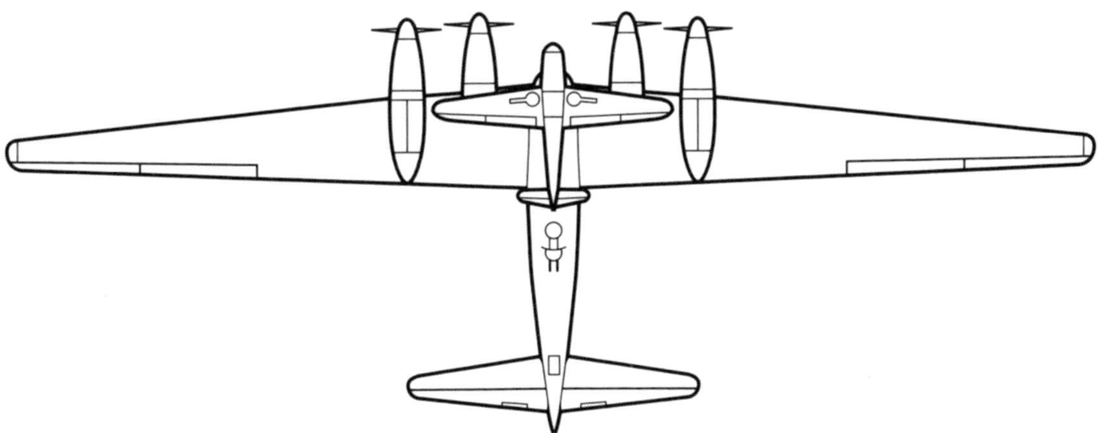

Another advanced idea which was heavily tested during the 1950s by the USAF was the 'parasite' fighter concept. The 'mother' aircraft in this case was the EF 101, which had a wingspan of 230ft and the ability to fly for 10,000 miles.

The swept-wing EF 132 bomber was the last project undertaken by Junkers before the Russians took over in 1945. One of many developments of the Ju 287, work on the project continued under Soviet control until 1948.

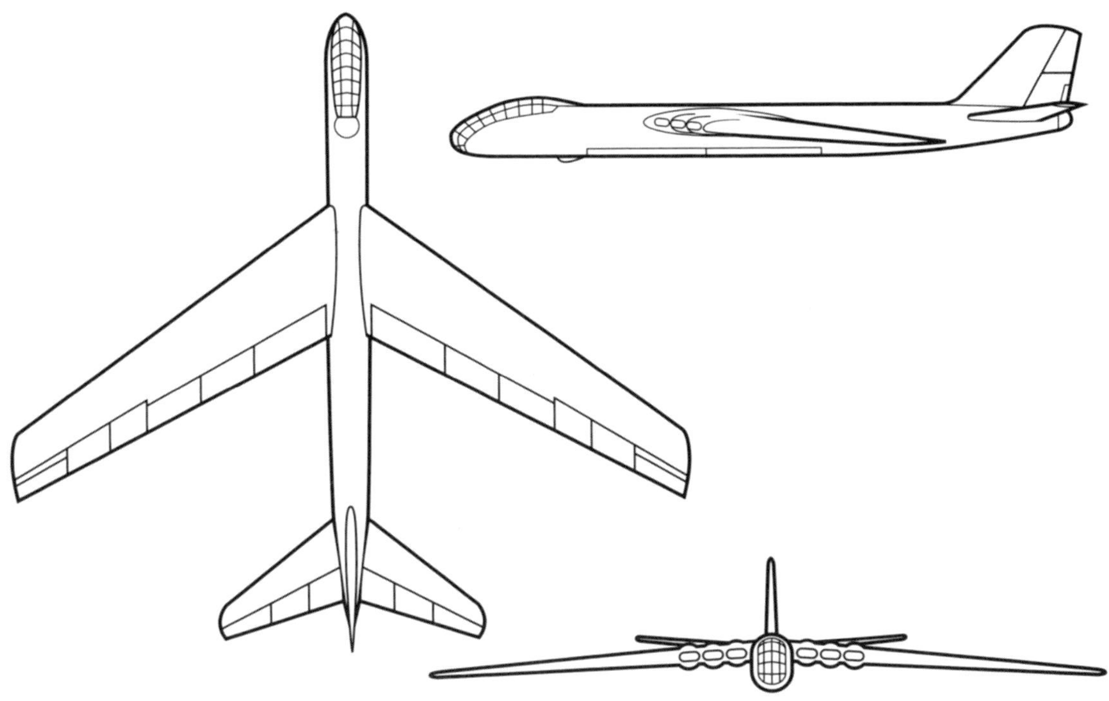

# Junkers Production 1915–45

| A/c | Type | First Flight | No | Service |
|-----|------|--------------|-----|---------|
| J 1 | Experimental | Dec 12, 1915 | 1 | |
| J 2 | Single-seat fighter | 1916 | 6-8 | |
| J 3 | Single-seat fighter | Not flown | 1 | |
| J 4 | Two-seat patrol | 1917 | 227 | Luftwaffe |
| J 7 | Single-seat fighter | Oct 1917 | 1 | |
| J 8 | Two-seat close support | Dec 26, 1916 | 4 | |
| J 9 | Single-seat fighter | Mar 10, 1918 | 41 | Geschwader Sachsenberg and Luftwaffe |
| J 10 | Two-seat ground attack | May 4, 1918 | 43 | (Civilian): Junkers-Luftverkehr; Lloyd-Luftverkehr Sablatnig. (Military): Geschwader Sachsenberg; Luftwaffe; Latvia AF and Soviet AF |
| J 11 | Two-seat fighter/recce | 1918 | 3 | German Navy |
| F 13 | Light transport | Jun 25, 1918 | 322 | (Civilian): Österreichische Luftverkehr AG (ÖLAG); Lloyd Aéreo Boliviano (LAB); Syndicato Condor; Varig; Bunavad; Avianco (SCADTA); Danziger Luftpost; Lloyd Ostflug; Aeronaut; Aero Airways; Kauhajoki Flying Club; Junkers Luftverkehr; Deutscher Aero Lloyd; Aeroexpress; Flugélag Íslands; Aero-Targ; Aerolloyd; Aerolot; LOT Polish Airlines; Serviços Aéreos Portugueses; Aviaarktika; South African Airways; Union Airways; As Astra Aero; Turkish Air Post; General Command of Mapping (Turkey) and the United States Post Office Dept. (Military): Afghan AF; Argentinian AF; Austria AF; Chilean AF; Bulgarian AF; Colombian AF; Finnish AF; Finnish Border Guard; Imperial Iranian AF; Lithuanian AF; Luftwaffe; Mongolian People's Army AF; Royal Air Force (64 AS (South Africa); Royal Romanian AF; Soviet AF, South African AF; Swedish AF; Turkish AF and the United States Navy. |

| A/c | Type | First Flight | No | Service |
|---|---|---|---|---|
| J 15 | Two-seat light mono | 1920 | 1 | |
| K 16 | General-Purpose transport | 1922 | 17 | Lufthansa; Weimar Engineering College; Junkers Luftverkehr; Stormbird ('Sturmuogel') Flying Assc.; Luftfrako; Deutraluft; Flughof G.m.b.H; |
| T 19 | Two-seat tourer | 1922 | 3 | |
| A 20 | Light transport | 1923 | 30* | Lufthansa; Junkers Luftverkehr; Soviet AF and Turkish AF. |
| H 21 | Recce monoplane | 1922 | 120* | Soviet AF; Aeroflot and Dobrolet |
| J 22 | Single-seat fighter | 1922 | 2 | Soviet AF |
| G 23 | Nine-seat airliner | 1924 | 15 | Ad Astra Aero; Aero Lloyd; Lufthansa; AB Flygindustri; Unión Aérea Española and ABA Schweden. |
| T 23 | Two-seat light a/c | 1923 | 4 | Fürth Flying School |
| F 24 | Single-eng G23/24 dev. | 1928 | 10* | Lufthansa |
| G 24 | Nine-seat airliner | 1925 | 56 | (Civilian): Syndicato Condor; Aero O/Y; Lufthansa, Condor Syndikat; AB Aerotransport; Ad Astra Aero; Swissair. (Military): Afghan AF; Austrian AF; Chilean AF; Luftwaffe; Hellenic AF; Spanish Republican AF; Turkish AF; Soviet AF and Yugoslav AF. |
| T 26 | Two-seat light aircraft | 1925 | 11* | F. Anhaltischer Aviation Assc. |
| T 27 | Two-seat light aircraft | 1925 | 1 | |
| T 29 | Two-seat tourer | 1925 | 2 | |
| K 30 | Medium/recce bomber | 1924 | 35 | Chilean Air Force (R42), Soviet Air Force (TB2/JuG-1), Spanish Air Force and Yugoslavian Air Force |
| G 31 | 15-seat/cargo airliner | 1926 | 13 | Lufthansa: Trust Territory of New Guinea (Guinea Airways), Bulolo Gold Dredging, RLM, Ölag and RAAF |
| A 32 | Three-seat experimental | 1926 | 2 | |
| W 33 | Medium cargo transport | 1926 | 199 | (Civilian): Syndicato Condor; Canadian Airways; SCADTA (Avianco); Lufthansa; Deruluft and Dobrolyot. (Military): Argentinian AF; Columbian AF; Ethiopian AF; Luftwaffe; Imperial Iranian AF; Mongolian People's Army AF; Swedish AF and Soviet AF. |

| A/c | Type | First Flight | No | Service |
| --- | --- | --- | --- | --- |
| W 34 | Six-seat airliner | 1926 | 3,000* | (Civilian): Syndicato Condor; Canadian Airways; SCADTA (Avianco); Lufthansa and South African Airways. (Military): Argentinian AF; Argentinian Navy; RAAF; Bolivian AF; Bulgarian AF; RCAF; Chilean AF; Chinese Nationalist AF; Colombia AF; Croatian AF; Czechoslovak AF; Finnish AF; Finnish Border Guard; Luftwaffe, Royal Norwegian AF; Papua New Guinea AF; Portuguese Army Aviation; Portuguese Naval Aviation; Slovak AF; Spanish AF; Swedish AF; SAAF and Venezuelan AF. |
| A 35 | Light transport | 1926 | 24 | Lufthansa; Chinese AF; Chilean AF; Soviet AF and Turkish AF |
| S 36 | Experimental bomber | 1927 | 1 | |
| K 37 | Bomber | 1928 | 2 | |
| Ki-1 | Bomber | 1932 | 219 | Japanese Air Force (K 37 variant) |
| Ki-2 | Bomber | 1933 | 126* | Japanese Air Force (K 37 variant) |
| G 38 | 34-seat airliner | Nov 6, 1929 | 2 | Lufthansa |
| K 39 | Experimental bomber | 1927 | 1 | (Converted for an A32 |
| K 43 | Recce monoplane | 1927 | 18 | Bolivian AF; Colombian AF; Finnish AF; Luftwaffe and Portuguese AF |
| Ju 46 | Mail floatplane | 1932 | 5 | Lufthansa |
| K 47 | Dive-bomber research | 1928 | 30* | Chinese AF and Luftwaffe |
| A 48 | K 47 prototype | 1927 | 1 | |
| Ju 49 | High-altitude research | Oct 2, 1931 | 1 | |
| A 50 | Two-seat sports tourer | 1929 | 69 | |
| K 51 | (Ki-20) Heavy bomber | 1934 | 6 | Japanese AF |
| Ju 52 | Medium cargo transport | Oct 13, 1930 | 6 | Canadian Pacific |
| Ju 52/3 | 15-seat airliner/ transport | May 1932 | 4,845 | (Civilian): Aero Cargo; Aero Oy; Aero Portuguesa; Aeroflot; Aeronorte; AGO; Air France; Air Ocean; Ala Littoria; British Airways; British European |

| A/c | Type | First Flight | No | Service |
|---|---|---|---|---|
| | | | | Airways; British Overseas Airways Corporation; Canadian Airways Ltd; Canadian Pacific Airlines; Compañía Aeroníutica Uruguaya S.A. (CAUSA); Cruzeiro; ČSA České aerolinie; CTA Languedoc Roussillon; Deruluft; Det Danske Luftartsselskab; Det Norske Luftfartselskap; Direccao de Exploracao dos Transportes Aéreos; DLL; Deutsche Lufthansa; Elliniki Eteria Enaerion Sinkinonion; Eurasia; Gibbes Sepik Airways; Iberia Airlines; JAT; Ju-Air; Lloyd Aéreo Boliviano; LOT Polish Airlines; Lufthansa; Malert Airlines; Mandated Airlines; Sabena; SCADTA; Société Auxiliare de Navigation Aérienne; Socotra; South African Airways; Swissair; Syndicato Condor (Serviços Aéreos Condor); VARIG; VASP. (Military): Air Force of the Independent State of Croatia; Argentinian AF; Austrian AF; Belgian AF; Bolivian AF; Bulgarian AF; Colombian AF; Czechoslovakian AF; Ecuadorian AF; Force Publique; French Air Force; French Navy; Hellenic AF; Luftwaffe; Norwegian AF; Peruvian AF; Portuguese AF; Regia Aeronautica; Romanian AF; Royal Air Force (British Airways Repair Unit (Middle East); Enemy Aircraft Servicing & Storage Flight; 83 Group Communication Flight; Fuhlsbüttel Station Flight, Gütersloh Station Flight); Royal Hungarian AF; Royal Norwegian Navy Air Service; Royal Romanian AF; SFR Yugoslav AF; Slovak AF; South African AF; Soviet AF; Spanish AF; Swedish AF and United States Army Air Forces (USAAF). |
| Ju 60 | High-speed airliner | 1932 | 2 | Deutsche Lufthansa and Luftwaffe |
| Ju 61 | (EF61) High-altitude research | 1936 | 2 | |

| A/c | Type | First Flight | No | Service |
| --- | --- | --- | --- | --- |
| Ju 86 | Medium airliner/ bomber | Nov 4, 1934 | 860* | (Civilian): AB Aerotransport; LAN Chile; Lloyd Aero Boliviano; Lufthansa; Manchukuo National Airways; South African Airways; Southern Airlines and Freighters of Australia and Swissair. (Military): Austrian AF; Bolivian AF; Chilean AF; Kempeitai; Luftwaffe; Portuguese AF; Romanian AF; Royal Hungarian AF; South African AF; Spanish AF and Swedish AF |
| Ju 87 | Dive bomber/ attack a/c | 1935 | 6,500* | Bulgarian AF; Czechoslovakian AF; Imperial Japanese AAF; Luftwaffe; Royal Hungarian AF; Regia Aeronautica; Royal Air Force; Royal Romanian AF; SFR Yugoslave AF; Slovenske Vzdusne Zbrane; Spanish Air Force; USAAF; Zrakoplovstvo Nezavisne Države Hrvatske (Croatia) |
| Ju 88 | High-speed bomber/fighter | Dec 21, 1936 | 15,183 | Bulgarian AF; Finnish AF; French AF, French Navy; Luftwaffe; Royal Air Force; Royal Hungarian AF; Soviet AF and Spanish AF |
| Ju 89 | Heavy bomber | 1936 | 1 | |
| Ju 90 | 38-40-seat airliner | Jun 7, 1937 | 19 | Deutsche Lufthansa and Luftwaffe |
| Ju 160 | High-speed airliner | Jun 1934 | 48 | Deutsche Lufthansa; Imperial Japanese Navy Air Service and Luftwaffe |
| Ju 188 | Medium bomber/ recce a/c | Sep 1941 | 1,606 | Aviation Navale; French AF; Luftwaffe and Royal Air Force |
| Ju 252 | Medium transport | 1941 | 15 | Luftwaffe |
| Ju 287 | Turbo-jet bomber | Feb 1945 | 23 | |
| Ju 288 | Medium bomber | Jan 41 | 18 | Luftwaffe |
| Ju 290 | Heavy transport/ recce a/c | 1941 | 68 | Luftwaffe |
| Ju 322 | Heavy transport glider | 1941 | 2 | |
| Ju 352 | Medium transport | 1944 | 50 | Luftwaffe |
| Ju 388 | Heavy fighter/recce a/c | 1943 | 100* | Luftwaffe |
| Ju 390 | Heavy long-rang transport | 1943 | 2 | |
| Mistel Composite | | 1943 | 210* | Luftwaffe |
| Ju 488 | High-altitude bomber | 1945 | 1 | Not flown |

Approximate total number of aircraft built = 34,238
*estimated

**Flt Lt 'Lew' Lewenden, Officer Commanding 1426 (Enemy Aircraft) Flight, at the controls of a Ju 88A at Collyweston in March 1944.**

With 4,845 built, the Ju 52 was one of the most successful transport aircraft ever manufactured. This is Junkers Ju 52 3/mfe D-2490 *Gustav Doerr* in service with Lufthansa in 1933. Re-registered as D-AFYS, the aircraft was transferred to the Luftwaffe in 1939 and is believed to have been written off in 1941.

2490